Dare to Soar

A Compilation

by

Jerry Cypher

Hummingbird World Media
Scenery Hill, Pennsylvania, USA

Hummingbird World Media
An Imprint of Double Edge Press

ISBN 978-1-938002-50-2

Dare to Soar
Copyright © 2015 Jerry Cypher

Non-Fiction

Dare to Soar

A Compilation

by

Jerry Cypher

Preface

Dare to Soar is a collection of works to provide readers the power of *faith, inspiration and hope.* As we embark on life's journey, this collection of works is a guide to keep our dreams alive and believe that all things are possible, even in our darkest days. It also attempts to inject a sense of perseverance, integrity and character into our daily lives.

Dare to Soar is never accidental. When we are confronted with life's challenges, we find ourselves at a crossroads of free will of choice. We decide how we move forward. Will we choose to be bitter or better, happy or sad, to act or avoid, succeed or fail, to believe or doubt?

The Bible teaches that wisdom begins with faith, fear in the Lord, and to trust Him in all things great and small. Wisdom! How does one gain wisdom and insight? It is through our lives' challenges and our reactions to them. If we choose to confront the adversity with an attitude of hope and faith and recognize that life gets messy, and that things happen *for* us not *to* us, we experience empowerment.

Holding onto our dreams and persevering through our fears, we develop a great sense of purpose and hope. It is my hope this book will provide the tools to help transform your thoughts, words, actions and habits to improve personal and spiritual growth.

Dare to Soar reaches individuals from all walks in life, from those who feel broken and defeated to the successful entrepreneur. It is an *Inspiration for Generations!*

~ *Jerry Cypher with Barbara Cypher*

About the Author

I am among all men blessed! In life, there are choices we make and events of which we have no control that mark us thereafter, e.g. Jacob's wrestling match with the angel. These choices and events shape the attitudes and form the character of who we are and what we become.

For me, the first event was Saturday, June 25, 1966. I faced adversity at eight years old when I lost my idol, mentor and best friend: my father. He was thirty-three when a heart attack took his life. This event affected me in the most positive way; albeit, during that time, I felt fear and uncertainty. We have heard, "but for the grace of God, go I." At the age of eight, the foundation of faith was ingrained in my being. By placing my life and trust in Jesus Christ, I shifted from a young boy to a young man with a desire to protect my mother, two sisters and younger brother. In the face of adversity, I am among all men blessed!

As you can imagine, there were financial difficulties: lack of money for the daily necessities, utility turn-off notices, and a near home foreclosure became part of my life experiences. I use the word 'experience' versus 'struggle' because I was rich in the important things of life. I was rich in having a loving and exceptionally close relationship with my mother and siblings, a supportive relationship with my extended family, and the neighborhood I grew up in, "Norwood," was the greatest place on earth. I am among all men blessed!

The second and most devastating life event happened April 28, 2014. My oldest son Brendan passed away at the age of twenty-nine. Though we are all saddened when we lose a parent, spouse, other family members and friends, the loss of a child is hard to find the words to describe. The dark, deep, relentless pain is a true test of faith.

I believe that all of us knows someone who is or has been victim to addiction. My son, Brendan, who over a decade of athletic injuries and surgeries was prescribed pain medication, which led to the ultimate tragedy of a mixture of prescription medicines taking his life.

Despite the testing of my faith, the deep, dark, relentless pain of burying our child, I still count myself as among all men, blessed! I am blessed for the close and quality relationship I had with Brendan. The love we shared for twenty-nine years was a beautiful bond that many men would need to live three lifetimes to experience.

I am blessed with the same close, quality, loving relationship with my remaining two sons, Jordan and Jerad. My wife Barbara is an inspiration to me, greatly beloved and my best friend. We share the same values in life and an unwavering faith. Ironically, her father also passed away when she was just a child of eleven. Again, with her by my side, I am among all men, blessed!

Professionally, I have been blessed to have fulfilled most of my dreams. I have built and owned multiple business ventures, including but not limited to a national and international employment-consulting firm, commercial and residential real estate, an entertainment company and a business brokerage firm. I am among all men, blessed!

Coaching has been my passion and ministry. I have been blessed to coach hundreds of young men at the college, high school and grade school levels. As a coach I had many roles: father, mother, disciplinarian, teacher, mentor, friend, psychologist, motivator, goal-setter, dreamer and minister

When I lost my son, Brendan, my gratitude to God never wavered. But I was not immune to the stages of grief. Shock. Anger. Depression. I asked the age-old question of God, "Why me?"

Eventually, I realized I was asking the wrong question. The question I needed to be asking was, "Why *not* me?"

God gave His only son so that the world may be saved. John 10:10 reads: "I have come to give you life, so you may have it abundantly." He didn't mean in material possessions; he meant it in love, forgiveness, compassion and grace. He didn't promise our lives would not have times of troubles, struggles and darkness. But if we turn to Him, He will bring us through darkness to the light. While I am processing the virtue of acceptance, my faith encourages me to move forward.

As I speak for me and my family, we are forever changed. We will choose to be better for this loss. We have been blessed as a family to reach out to others who may need a word of encouragement, a spark of hopefulness, and compassion. It is my hope this collection of works that have resonated in my life will resonate in yours as well, and you will be forever changed.

I am among all men, blessed!

~ *Jerry Cypher*

Table of Contents

I

THE WISDOM OF GOD

God without man is still God.

Man without God is nothing.

Who is God? What is His name? He is what He has done for us. To know God we must discover what he had to say about himself. Open the Scriptures; look around at creation; feel life happening to us. We might not be able to explain life's ultimate meaning; words are so very limited. But eventually we hear ourselves whisper: God.

God once told us His name. He said: "I am who I am." He tells us, in effect, that where everything is, there I am. I am where you are, what you do, what you feel, and what you see.

Butterflies

One day a small opening appeared on a cocoon. A man sat and watched the butterfly for several hours as it struggled to force its body through that little hole. Then it seemed to stop making progress. It appeared as if it had gotten as far as it could and it could go no further.

So the man decided to help the butterfly. He took a pair of scissors and snipped off the remaining bit of the cocoon. The butterfly then emerged easily, but it had a swollen body and small shriveled wings.

The man continued to watch the butterfly because he expected that, at any moment, the wings would enlarge and expand to be able to support the body which would contract in time. Neither happened! In fact, the butterfly spent the rest of its life crawling around with a swollen body and shriveled wings. It never was able to fly.

What the man in his kindness and haste to help did not understand was that the restricting cocoon and the struggle required for the butterfly to get through the tiny opening was God's way of forcing fluid from the body of the butterfly into its wings so that it would be ready for flight once it achieved its freedom from the cocoon.

Sometimes struggles are exactly what we need in life. If God allowed us to go through our life without any obstacles, it would cripple us. We would not be as strong as what we could have been. We could never fly.

I asked for Strength. . . and God gave me Difficulties to make me strong.

I asked for Wisdom. . . and God gave me Problems to solve.

I asked for Prosperity. . . and God gave me Brain and Brawn to work.

I asked for Courage. . . and God gave me Danger to overcome.

I asked for Love. . . and God gave me Troubled people to help.

I asked for Favors. . . and God gave me Opportunities.

I received nothing I asked for. . . I received everything I needed.

❖

Proverbs 3

Further Benefits of Wisdom

My son, do not forget my teaching, but keep my commands in your heart, for they will prolong your life many years and bring you prosper-ity.

Let love and faithfulness never leave you; bind them around your neck. Write them on the tablet of your heart. Then you will win favor and a good name in the sight of God and man.

Trust in the Lord with all your heart and lean not on your own under-standing; in all your ways acknowledge him, and he will make your paths straight.

Do not be wise in your own eyes; fear the Lord and shun evil. This will bring health to your body and nourishment to your bones.

Honor the Lord with your wealth, with the first fruits of all your crops; then your barns will be filled to overflowing, and your vats will brim over with new wine.

My son, do not despise the Lord's discipline and do not resent his rebuke, because the Lord disciplines those he loves, as a father the son he delights in.

Blessed is the man who finds wisdom, for the man who gains under-standing, for she is more profitable than silver and yields better returns than gold. She is more precious than rubies; nothing you desire can com-pare with her. Long life is in her right hand; in her left hand are riches and honor. Her ways are pleasant ways, and all her paths are peace. She is a tree of life to those who embrace and those who lay hold of her will be blessed.

By wisdom the Lord laid the earth's foundations, by understanding he set the heavens in place; by his knowledge the deeps were divided, and the clouds let drop the dew.

My son, preserve sound judgment and discernment, do not let them out of your sight; they will be life for you, an ornament to grace your neck. Then you will go on your way in safety, and your foot will not stumble; when you lie down, you will not be afraid; when you lie down, your sleep will be sweet. Have no fear of sudden disaster or of the ruin that overtakes the wicked, for the Lord will be your confidence and will keep your foot from being snared.

Do not withhold good from those who deserve it, when it is in your power to act. Do not say to your neighbor, "Come back later; I'll give it tomorrow"—when you now have it with you.

Do not plot harm against your neighbor, who lives trustfully near you. Do not accuse a man for no reason—when he has done you no harm.

Do not envy a violent man or choose any of his ways, for the Lord detests a perverse man but takes the upright into his confidence.

The Lord's curse is on the house of the wicked, but he blesses the home of the righteous. He mocks proud mockers but gives grace to the humble. The wise inherit honor, but fools he holds up to shame.

Footprints in the Sand

One night a man had a dream. He dreamed he was walking along the beach with the Lord. Across the sky flashed scenes from his life. For each scene he noticed two sets of footprints in the sand; one belonging to him, and the other to the Lord.

When the last scene flashed before him, he looked back at the footprints and noticed that many times along the path there was only one set of footprints in the sand. He also noticed that this happened during the lowest and saddest times in his life.

This really bothered him so he questioned the Lord.

"Lord, you said that once I decided to follow you, you would walk with me all the way, but I noticed that during the most troublesome times of my life, there was only one set of footprints. I don't understand why, when I needed you the most, you deserted me."

The Lord replied, "My precious, precious child, I love you and would never leave you. During your times of trial and suffering, when you see only one set of footprints, it was then that I carried you."

~ Author Unknown

The Beatitudes

Now when he saw the crowds, he went on a mountainside and sat down. His disciples came to him, ²and he began to say to them, saying:
³"Blessed are the poor in spirit, for theirs is the kingdom of heaven.
⁴Blessed are those who mourn, for they will be comforted.
⁵Blessed are the meek, for they will inherit the earth.
⁶Blessed are those who hunger and thirst for righteousness, for they will be filled.
⁷Blessed are the merciful, for they will be shown mercy.
⁸Blessed are the pure in heart, for they will see God.
⁹Blessed are the peacemakers, for they will be called sons of God.
¹⁰Blessed are those who are persecuted because of righteousness, for theirs is the kingdom of heaven."

A Time for Everything

There is a time for everything, and a season for every activity under heaven:
²a time to be born and a time to die, a time to plant and a time to uproot,
³a time to kill and a time to heal, a time to tear down and a time to build,
⁴a time to weep and a time to laugh, a time to mourn and a time to dance,
⁵a time to scatter stones and a time to gather them, a time to embrace and a time to refrain,
⁶a time to search and a time to give up, a time to keep and a time to throw away,
⁷a time to tear and a time to mend, a time to be silent and at time to speak,
⁸a time to love, a time to hate, a time for war and a time for peace.

❖

Gifts of the Heart

Gold and Silver are gifts that are treasured by many. . . But the *Gifts of the Heart* cost not a penny.

A smile is a gift you can give every day. A letter is a gift to a friend who's away.

Laughter is a gift that holds happiness in it. Time is a gift to enjoy every minute.

Some people like the gift of advice. It's just a gift to say, "I like you! You're nice!"

A quarrel patched up is a special gift. And so is giving someone a lift.

A task is a gift that can be fun. And praise is a gift for a job well done.

"Thank you's" and "Please's" and "Yes'es" are gifts. But seldom give "Oh, no's" or "Maybe's" or "If's."

We sometimes find gifts in the strangest of places. . . like old trunks . . . and old trees. . . and very shy faces.

The world is a gift! For God, in His love, gives us green meadows and blue skies above.

Giving is receiving. Receiving is giving! That's really the secret that lies behind living.

So. . . Give something each day and you will see that it's true. . .

All the *Gifts of the Heart* shall be given to you.

Things to Think About

An elderly gentleman passed his granddaughter's room one night and overheard her repeating the alphabet in an oddly reverent way. "What on earth are you up to?" he asked.

"I'm saying my prayers," explained the little girl. "But I can't think of exactly the right words tonight, so I'm just saying all the letters. God will put them together for me, because he knows what I'm thinking.

❖

One day a friend of Samuel Morse, inventor of the telegraph, said to him, "Professor, when you were making your experiments, did you ever come to a place not knowing what to do next?"

"More than once," Morse replied, "and whenever I could not see my way clearly, I knelt down and prayed to God for light and understand-ing."

Then Morse added: "When flattering honors came to me from America and Europe on account of my invention, I never felt I deserved them. I had made a valuable application of electricity, not because I was superior to other men, but solely because God, who meant it for man-kind, must reveal it to someone, and it pleased him to reveal it to me."

In May 1844, the first message to be sent over the telegraph, dispatched by Morse himself between Washington and Baltimore, were the words: "What hath God wrought!"

An optimist goes to the window every morning and says, "Good morning, God."

The pessimist goes to the window and says, "Good God, morning!"

A Rabbi was walking down the street when a member of his congregation came along and boasted that he had read all the volumes of the Talmud three times.

The rabbi looked at him and said, *"The important thing is not how many times you have been through the Talmud, but whether the Talmud has been through you."*

God gave us two ears but only one mouth. Some people say that's because he wanted us to spend twice as much time listening as talking. Others claim it's because he knew listening was twice as hard as talking.

Our life is torn with such trivia that we need a unity or pattern of growth that will 'put it together." Prayer puts the pieces together.

It creates a hum – something that will hold everything together as our ideas and feelings go off in different directions.

As we enter the mental decompression chamber of our own mind to relax and unwind, our prayer can be as simple as only saying the name of God. We might not wish to talk, but we can listen as our thoughts and dreams reveal his response. We'll begin to feel the vibrations of his presence as we would with anyone who loves us so much.

❖

There is a story told of how God chose to reveal himself to a little girl: "Hi, I'm God," he said. "Do you know who I am?"

"Sure," said the girl. "You are the eschatological entity, the Alpha and Omega, the infinite being that is omnipotent and eternal."

And God answered: "Are you sure you have the right person?"

Language searches for adjectives that will describe God. We complicate him with titles and attributes that have filled volumes. God is found in simplicity.

❖

When we break a branch off a vine, it shrivels and the grapes dry up like raisins.

It loses its vitality and sustenance.

Jesus Christ testified this would happen when he said: "Remain in union with me and I will remain in union with you. Unless you remain in me you cannot bear fruit, just as a branch cannot bear fruit unless it re-mains on the vine. I am the vine, you are the branches and so without me you can do nothing."

If you feel like a dried-up raisin, then seek out the ultimate experience – meet God in prayer.

❖

Jesus said: "My peace I give to you. My peace I leave with you;" then he submitted himself to suffering. He didn't suppress, explain, or justify it.

Suffering offers a detachment and transcendence. It makes all our material possessions seem unimportant and frees us to go beyond them and find the real value of living.

Nervousness, restlessness, anxiety, yawning, running eyes, sweating, "gooseflesh," muscle twitching, hot and cold flashes, severe aches of back and legs, vomiting, diarrhea, and a feeling of desperation: All these complications characterize a withdrawal from opiates. What great joy – a momentary escape from reality only to face new problems!

Recreation "creates again." It refreshes the mind, renews the spirit, and motivates the body. Activity can go wild unless we control it by integrating it with rest and relaxation.

Everyone needs a quiet center within himself—like the depth of the ocean. When a hurricane comes the fish go to the bottom of the ocean and wait it out. If we develop a desire for silence in our life we can wait out many problems—not by escaping but by pausing and absorbing.

God gave us two ears and one mouth with the intention, probably, that we listen twice as much as we speak. Ideas happen when we quietly and humbly listen.

G. K. Chesterton said: "Thinking means connecting things." This assimilation requires a certain amount of silence. Ideas breathe in solitude. They expand and envision new horizons. Silence opens up a life that activity has little time or energy to discover.

We cannot call upon faith unless we have developed its strength and intelligence with prayer.

Faith does not come from will power; it is a gift of God's love in response to our deep relationship with him. We cannot create faith when we need it. We must already have it, and prayer keeps it fresh and vibrant.

❖

Prayer not only gives answers, it also gives direction. It offers a good fusion point for our ideas and feelings to meet and settle differences.

It settles the mind and emotions by quieting the spirit, and then proceeds to overcome our anxieties, guilt complexes, and inferiorities by refreshing our faith, assuring forgiveness, and convincing us of our special dignity before God.

Jesus eulogized excellence at the Last Supper: *I have given you glory on earth by finishing the work you gave me to do. Do you now, Father, give me glory at your side, a glory I had with you before the world began.* (John 17:4, 5)

Cardinal Suenens describes the full meaning of shalom when he said:

"The greatest good we can do for others is not to give them of our wealth but to show them their own."

Shalom brings us beyond the horizon of our own ideas and idiosyncrasies. We begin to tolerate other people. We do not attempt to form them into our shadow. We encourage them to develop their own talents. They have a fullness and potential all of their own. We might not agree with their ideas or life style but at least we are happy that they are becoming themselves.

I'm sure Jesus greeted others with the word "Shalom," which not only means peace but also wholeness and fullness. Shalom hopes the very best for a person. It is difficult for us to enjoy everyone, but we can hope that each receives the best of what life offers.

The amount of time spent praying is not essential. Prayer can be instant and spontaneous with the simplicity of just turning our heart and mind to the presence of God.

The Old Testament people did not have a word for prayer. They used the words 'sing', 'rejoice', 'laugh', and 'dance'. Prayer became the culmination of their total human experience—given to God. Everything they said or did for God was a prayer.

It should be likewise with us. We live to praise God. So the more we appreciate, celebrate, and recreate life around us, the more we praise God.

God is often part of our pension and Medicare plan because we feel we must have time and leisure to pray. It is certainly preferable that we do enjoy solitude for prayer but this is a luxury. Ordinarily we will find time to talk to God as we talk to people—when we are busy.

God is a Someone—more to be met than analyzed. He is as close to us as our desire to see him, for he revealed himself as "God is with us." St. James tells us, "come near to God and he will come near to us."

St. Paul says: "God is not far from any one of us. For in him we live and move and have our being."

"God, what is your name?" we all ask—hoping, like Moses, to capture the meaning of being God. But we will always be frustrated unless we stop talking about *a* god and begin to address him as *my* God.

❖

The little child in the warmth and comfort of his mother's body is afraid to be born. He has no idea what this other life will be like. Perhaps it is that same fear that we anticipate in death. Unless that child is born, however, he will never feel the love of his parents, see the colors of nature, and enjoy the beauty of sunlight.

Even though we experience many difficulties in this early life, we enjoy the comfort of security in the womb of mother earth. We know what we have, and we are afraid to risk the unknown. We feel the same fear as that nine-month-old child in his mother's womb. Unless we are born again in death, however, we'll never experience our greatest happiness.

If we look back over our life, we'll find it hard to realize that we have allowed so many small disappointments to worry us in such a big way. With a sense of proportion, we'll never let it happen again.

❖

There is nothing so overwhelming that we cannot handle, but for extra help we could make this prayer a daily experience:

O Lord, help me to remember that nothing is going to happen to me today that you and I together cannot handle.

❖

What does a person feel in his first experience of eternity? What does he see? What has God prepared for him? If we could revive his human life, would he opt to come back? Is eternity too wonderful to ever return to time? We all wish to know, but we do not want to die to find out.

Death is not *something that happens to us* but a *person who is met.* We will not be afraid of this beautiful experience that awaits us if we are not afraid of God.

❖

We must come to realize that there are some mysteries we cannot answer, some problems we cannot solve, some situations that we will never find agreeable, but we can be happy in spite of them. The secret word is acceptance. If we can do something about the problem, fine. If we cannot, then we accept it and learn to live with it. Reinhold Niebuhr has written a beautiful prayer that we should make our own:

God grant me SERENTIY to accept the things I cannot change, COUR-AGE to change the things I can, and WISDOM to know the difference.

❖

Three Bullets

There once was a man who had nothing for his family to eat. He had an old rifle and three bullets. So, he decided that he would go out hunting and kill some wild game for dinner. As he went down the road, he saw a rabbit. He shot at the rabbit and missed. The rabbit ran away.

Then he saw a squirrel and fired a shot at the squirrel and missed it. The squirrel disappeared into a hole in a cottonwood tree.

As he went further, he saw a large wild "Tom" turkey in the tree, but he had only one bullet remaining. A voice spoke to him and said, "Pray first, aim high and stay focused."

However, at the same time, he saw a deer which was a better kill. He brought the gun down and aimed at the deer. He then saw a rattlesnake between his legs about to bite him, so he naturally brought the gun down further to shoot the rattlesnake.

Still, the voice said again to him, "I said, pray, aim high and stay focused." So, the man decided to listen to God's voice. He prayed, then aimed the gun high up in the tree and shot the wild turkey. The bullet passed thru the turkey and killed the deer. The handle fell off the gun and hit the snake in the head and killed it.

Live in Peace

"If it is possible, as far as it depends on you, live at peach with everyone." (Romans 12:18 NIV)

Did you know there is strength in living at peace? That is why the Lord commands that we live at peach with those around us. When there is strife and contention, then the enemy has an open door to move in your life. But when we are at peace with those around us, we are in a position of strength. Being at peace with those around you doesn't mean you have to agree with everyone. It simply means you are walking in love. It means you are patient and kind, not envious, not boastful. It means you are considerate, kind, and gracious because of what the Lord has done in your heart. If you need peace today, ask the Lord to fill your heart so that you can extend peace to those around you. As you do, you'll live in a position of strength and walk in the daily blessing the Lord has in store for you!

Dear Lord, thank You for the gift of peace which is strength. Today, I choose to release any strife or contention in my heart. I ask You to fill me with Your peace so that I can be an instrument of Your glory in the earth, in Jesus' name. Amen.

II

GUIDE TO SURVIVING THE TEEN YEARS ~ AND BEYOND

Watch your thoughts; they become words.

Watch your words; they become actions.

Watch your actions; they become habits.

Watch your habits; they become character.

Watch your character; it becomes your destiny.

~ Frank Outlaw

Believe It Or Not

In the 1940's, a survey listed the top seven discipline problems in public schools: talking, chewing gum, making noise, running in the halls, getting out of line, wearing improper clothes, and not putting paper in wastebaskets. A more recent survey lists these top seven: drug abuse, alcohol abuse, pregnancy, suicide, rape, robbery, and assault. (Arson, gang warfare, and venereal disease are also–rans.)

~ George F. Will

DON'T WAIT for the inspired moments; work every day or you may miss them. Little by little you may find that your best work in a sense creates itself, your hands functioning almost without conscious control. You may come to wonder how much is really yours and how much mysteriously part of some universal force.

~ Wheeler Williams

A research organization, making a study of juvenile delinquency, telephoned fifty homes between 9:30 and 10:30 at night to ask parents if they knew where their children were. Half of the calls were answered by children who had no idea where their parents were.

If you don't know where you are going, every road will get you nowhere.   ~ Henry Kissinger

Monday: I was walking down Main Street. There was a big hole. I fell in. This was not my fault.
Tuesday: I was walking down Main Street. There was a big hole. I

pretended not to see it. I closed my eyes, and I fell in. This was not my fault.

Wednesday: I was walking down Main Street. There was a big hole. I saw it. I fell in, and this is now a bad habit.

Thursday: I was walking down Main Street. There was a big hole. I walked around it.

Friday: I have chosen to walk down a different street.

The Morals of the Story

1. The road to success is narrow, but big is the hole that leads to failure.
2. Master your habits and your attitude or they will master you.
3. You have the power over the choices you make; use them wisely.

~ Coach Jerry Cypher

Teen Commandments

1. Don't let your parents down; They brought you up.
2. Choose your companions with care; You become what they are.
3. Be master of your habits; Or they will master you.
4. Treasure your time; Don't spend it; invest it
5. Stand for something; Or you'll fall for anything.
6. Select only a date; Who would make a good mate.
7. See what you can do for others; Not what others can do for you.
8. Guard your thoughts; What you think, you are.
9. Don't fill up on this world's crumbs; Feed your soul on the Living Bread.
10. Give your all to Christ; He gave His all for you.

~ Author Unknown

Ten Rules Kids won't Learn in School

1. Life is not fair. Get used to it. The average teenager uses the phrase "It's not fair" 86 times a day.

2. The real world won't care as much about your self-esteem as your school does. This may come as a shock.
3. Sorry, you won't make $40,000 a year right out of high school. And you won' be a vice president; you may even have to wear a uniform that doesn't have a designer label.
4. If you think your teacher is tough, wait until you get a boss.
5. Flipping burgers is not beneath your dignity. Your grandparents had a different word for burger flipping. They called it opportunity.
6. It's not your parents' fault if you mess up. You're responsible. This is the flip side of "It's my life" and "You're not my boss."
7. Before you were born, your parents weren't boring. They got that way paying your bills and listening to you.
8. Life is not divided into semesters. And you don't get summers off—not even spring break. You are expected to show up every day for eight hours, and you don't get a new life every 10 weeks.
9. Smoking does not make you look cool. Watch an 11-year old with a butt in his mouth. That's what you look like to anyone over 20.
10. Your school may be 'outcome-based', but life isn't. In some schools, you're given as many times as you want to get the answer right. Standards are set low enough so everyone can meet them. This, of course, bears not the slightest resemblance to anything in real life—as you will find out. Good luck. You are going to need it—and the harder you work, the luckier you will get.

~ Ann Landers

Thomas Jefferson's Decalogue for the Practical Life

1. Never put off till tomorrow what you can do today.
2. Never trouble another for what you can do yourself.
3. Never spend your money before you have it.
4. Never buy what you do not want because it is cheap.
5. Pride costs us more than hunger, thirst and cold.
6. We never repent of having eaten too little.
7. Nothing is troublesome that we do willingly.
8. How much pain has cost us the evils that have never happened?

9. Take things always by their smooth handle.
10. When angry, count ten before you speak; if very angry, a hundred.

~ Thomas Jefferson

25 Things You'll Need to Know After High School

1. Don't sweat the small stuff, and remember, most stuff is small.
2. The most boring word in any language is "I."
3. Nobody is indispensable, especially you.
4. Life is full of surprises. Just say "never" and you'll see.
5. People are more important than things.
6. Persistence will get you almost anything eventually.
7. Nobody can make you happy. Most folks are about as happy as they make up their minds to be.
8. There's so much bad in the best of us and so much good in the worst of us that it doesn't behoove any of us to talk about the rest of us.
9. Live by what you trust, not by what you fear.
10. Character counts. Family matters.
11. Laugh every day, even at yourself.
12. If you wait to have kids until you can afford them, you probably never will.
13. Baby kittens don't begin to open their eyes for six weeks after birth, some people 26 years.
14. The world would run a lot smoother if more men knew how to dance.
15. Television ruins more minds than drugs.
16. Sometimes there is more to gain in being wrong than right.
17. Life is so much simpler when you tell the truth.
18. People who do the world's real work don't usually wear neckties.
19. A good joke beats a pill for a lot of ailments.
20. There are no substitutes for fresh air, sunshine and exercise.
21. A smile is the cheapest way to improve your looks, even if your teeth are crooked.

22. May you live life so there is standing room only at your funeral.
23. Mothers always know best, but sometimes fathers know, too.
24. Forgive yourself, your friends and your enemies. You're all only human.
25. If you don't do anything else in life, love someone and let someone love you.

Top 20 Excuses for Not Getting Anything Done

1. It's no fun
2. It's not due yet
3. I work better under pressure
4. It will take care of itself
5. It's too early to worry about it
6. It's too late to worry about it
7. I'm not ready
8. It's too hard
9. I don't feel like it right now
10. I have a headache
11. It won't matter if it's a little late
12. It may be important but it isn't urgent
13. It might hurt
14. I really mean to do it, but I keep forgetting
15. If I put it off, somebody else might do it
16. It might be embarrassing
17. I'm too tired
18. I'm too busy right now
19. I've got to tidy up first
20. I need to sleep on it

HELP YOUR GRADES

Study—Do Homework
Take Notes
Be First in Class
Be Last to Leave Class
Sit Up Front
Do Not Yawn Acting Bored
Do Not Look at Your Watch/Clock
Look Interested
Be Attentive
Ask Questions
Know What the Teacher's Expectations Are
Go Along with the Teacher's Style of Teaching
Get Help from Good Students/Tutors/Teachers
Organize Your Time

Study Demands:

1. Emphasis should be on quest and attainment of knowledge, not grades and credits.
2. Never miss or be late for any class or appointment.
3. Have regular study hours and keep them.
4. Get your work in on time and do not fall behind.
5. If you need extra help in your studies, let your teacher/coach/someone know. Most instructors are willing and happy to help, but you must make the first contact.
6. Take advantage of all the available educational resources (library services, computer labs, reading labs, counseling center, etc.).
7. When you are to miss school because of basketball, please contact the instructors of the classes you will miss beforehand, and tell them that you will be absent, and request assignments for those dates.
8. Do not expect favors or special treatment. Do your part!

ORGANIZING MY LIFE

TO DO: DATE:

BUSINESS: **MESSAGES:**

1. _____	1. _____
2. _____	2. _____
3. _____	3. _____
4. _____	4. _____
5. _____	5. _____
6. _____	6. _____
7. _____	7. _____

PERSONAL:

1. _____	8. _____
2. _____	9. _____
3. _____	10. _____
	11. _____

APPOINTMENTS:

5:30 a.m. _____	2:00 p.m. _____
6:00 a.m. _____	2:30 p.m. _____
6:30 a.m. _____	3:00 p.m. _____
7:00 a.m. _____	3:30 p.m. _____
7:30 a.m. _____	4:00 p.m. _____
8:00 a.m. _____	4:30 p.m. _____
8:30 a.m. _____	5:00 p.m. _____
9:00 a.m. _____	5:30 p.m. _____
9:30 a.m. _____	6:00 p.m. _____
10:00 am. _____	6:30 p.m. _____
10:30 am. _____	7:00 p.m. _____
11:00 am. _____	7:30 p.m. _____
11:30 am. _____	8:00 p.m. _____
12:00 p.m. _____	8:30 p.m. _____
12:30 p.m. _____	9:00 p.m. _____
1:00 p.m. _____	9:30 p.m. _____
1:30 p.m. _____	10:00 p.m. _____

The More Things Change, the More They Stay the Same

The thoughts that come often unsought and, as it were, drop into the mind are the most valuable of any we have, and therefore, should be secured because they seldom return again.

~ John Locke

Happiness does not come from possessions, but from our appreciation of them. It does not come from our work, but from our attitude toward that work. It does not come from success, but from the growth we attain in achieving that success.

Time is the one thing we all possess. Our success depends upon the proper use of our time and its by-product, the odd moment.

Every minute that you save by making it useful or more profitable is that much added to your life and its possibilities. Every minute lost is a neglected by-product—once gone, you will never get it back.

Think of the odd quarter of an hour before breakfast, the odd half hour after lunch. Remember the chance to read, or figure, or think with concentration about your own career, that presents itself now and again during the day. All of these opportunities are the by-products of your daily existence. Use them and you may find what many successful companies have found that real profit is in the utilization of the by-products.

Among the aimless, unsuccessful, or worthless, you often hear talk about 'killing time'. Those who are always killing time are really killing their chances in life. Those who are destined to become successful are those who make time by making it useful.

~ Arthur Brisbane

When you look in your mirror in the morning and congratulate yourself on your nimble brain, consider this:

The light over your mirror was perfected by a man who was virtually deaf. While your radio plays, remember the hunchback who helped invent it. If you listen to contemporary music, you may hear an artist who is blind. If you prefer classical, you may enjoy a symphony written by a composer who couldn't hear. One of the foremost presidents of the United States could hardly walk. A woman born unable to see, speak, or hear stands as a great achiever. The handicapped can enrich our lives. Let's enrich theirs.

~ From an ad by United Technologies Corporation

We must prepare ourselves by study and know far more than we impart if we expect to convey accurate and responsible ideas.

What we do not have, we cannot give; to act without knowledge only causes confusion.

Quiet reflection dissolves vague uncertainty. Our ideology should be like an iceberg—more ideology below than shown above.

Organization saves our energy and does not waste our valuable time on nonessentials, overlap, or misdirection. The few hours we spend each week in ordering and preparing our activities will give us the sense of priority and proportion we need to stay in control of our life and conserve our energy.

Organization also gives us the gift of patience and tolerance. We are easily frustrated. But frustration without tolerance becomes imprudent aggression, which seeks immediate relief. We strike out in anger to relieve the tension and dissipate our energy with bullying, hostility, revenge, and violence.

Everyone needs a few close friends with whom to share intimate thoughts and to entrust secrets. Unfortunately, we cannot develop this closeness with everyone, so we must choose. Of all our friends, who will help us to become more appreciative of life and more enthusiastic about celebrating its wonders?

A friend should be chosen slowly and very carefully. As George Washington warned:

> "Be courteous to all, but intimate with few,
> And let those few be well tried,
> Before you give them your confidence.
> True friendship is a plant of slow growth."

> I became a friend and my spirit whispered:
> Here's my life, come and make it beautiful
> Here's my life. You have the power to change me
> Here's my life, you have the chance to hurt me
> Here's my life, make it better than I would.
> If we cry in self-pity, "No one cares about me,"
> perhaps it is our own fault.

We cannot buy the belonging of love. It is something we receive after sharing and spending ourselves. We must be persons who love before we can expect to be loved.

The founder of a highly successful company was asked what it took to succeed. "The same thing it took to get started," he replied, "a sense of urgency about getting things done."

The people who make things move in this world share this same sense of urgency. No matter how intelligent or able you may be, if you don't have this sense of urgency, now is the time to start developing it. The world is full of very competent people who honestly intend to do things tomorrow, or as soon as they can get to it. Their accomplishments, however, seldom match those of the less talented who are blessed with a sense of the importance of getting started now.

~ Henry Ford

One of the sanest, surest, and most generous joys of life comes from being happy over the good fortune of others.

To handle yourself, use your head; to handle others, use your heart.
~ Donald Laird

An idealist believes the short run doesn't count; a cynic believes the long run doesn't matter. A realist believes that what was done or left undone in the short run determines the long run.
~ Sydney J. Harris

How much you do is important. How well you do it is decisive.

We're told that if you take the Pali Highway northbound out of Honolulu, you'll discover something that a lot of people who have never been to Hawaii found out long ago.

When you get to the Pali Pass, turn right on Park Street. Go one block and you come to Easy Street. Turn left and go one more block. There you'll see a sign that says Dead End.

The crown of all faculties is common sense. It is not enough to do the right thing; it must be done at the right time and place. Talent knows what do to; tact knows when and how to do it.
~ William Matthews

❖

You can buy a man's time; you can buy his physical presence at a given place; you can even buy a measured number of his skilled muscular motions per hour. But you cannot buy enthusiasm. . . you cannot buy loyalty. . . you cannot buy devotion of hearts, minds, or souls. You must earn these.

~ Clarence Francis

Humanity certainly needs practical people who get the most out of their work and, without forgetting the general good, safeguard their own interests. But humanity also needs dreamers, for whom the development of an enterprise is so captivating that it becomes possible for them to devote their own material profit.

❖

Wonderment, curiosity and adventure are the vital signs of an interesting life. When we are interested in the many experiences of life, each day is a challenge. We awake with the thrilling feeling of learning something new, and fulfilling something we could not accomplish yesterday.

Interest must come from our own impetus, however. We create it with pure desire and participation. It grows from the feeling that we have a contribution to make so we will not let this day pass without accomplishing something.

We tap our potential every time we think and humbly say: "I know that I do not know." We no longer pretend to be already fulfilled, so we yearn for the opportunity to listen and learn.

In moods of doubt and frustration in the face of injustice and wretchedness, I think of the counsel of the most sagacious man I have ever known, Justice Branseis. "My dear," he once advised his impatient daughter, "if you would only recognize that life is hard, things would be so much easier for you."

~ Paul A. Freund

Ours seems to be the only nation on earth that asks its teenagers what to do about world affairs and tells it golden-agers to go out and play.

~ Julian Gerow

❖

Dead at Seventeen

Agony claws my mind. I am a statistic. When I first got here, I felt very much alone. I was overwhelmed by grief, and I expected to find sympathy.

I found no sympathy. I saw only thousands of others whose bodies were as badly mangled as mine. I was given a number and placed in a category. The category was called "Traffic Fatalities."

The day I died was an ordinary day. How I wish I had taken the bus! But I was too cool for the bus. I remember how I wheedled the car from Mom. "Special favor," I pleaded. "All the kids drive." When the 2:50 p.m. bell rang, I threw my books in the locker. . . free until tomorrow morning! I ran to the parking lot, excited at the thought of driving a car and being my own boss.

It doesn't matter how the accident happened. I was goofing off—going too fast, taking crazy chances. But I was enjoying my freedom and having fun. The last thing I remember was passing an old lady who seemed to be going awfully slow. I heard a crash and felt a terrific jolt. Glass and steel flew everywhere. My whole body seemed to be turning inside out. I heard myself scream.

Suddenly, I awakened. It was very quiet. A police officer was standing over me. I saw a doctor. My body was mangled. I was saturated with blood. Pieces of jagged glass were sticking out all over. Strange, I couldn't feel anything.

Hey, don't pull that sheet over my head! I can't be dead. I'm only seventeen. I've got a date tonight. I'm supposed to have a wonderful life ahead of me. I haven't lived yet. I can't be dead.

Later, I was placed in a drawer. My folks came to identify me. Why did they have to see me like this? Why did I have to look at Mom's eyes when she faced the most terrible ordeal of her life? Dad suddenly looked very old. He told the man in charge, "Yes, he's our son."

The funeral was weird. I saw all of my relatives and friends walk toward the casket. They looked at me with the saddest eyes I've ever seen. Some of my buddies were crying. A few of the girls touched my hand and sobbed as they walked by.

Please, somebody—wake me up! Get me out of here. I can't bear to see Mom and Dad in such pain. My grandparents are so weak from grief they can barely walk.

My brother and sister are like zombies. They move like robots, in a daze. Everybody, no one can believe this. I can't believe it, either.

Please, don't bury me! I'm not dead! I have a lot of living to do! I want to laugh and run again. I want to sing and dance. Please don't put me in the ground! I promise if you give me just one more chance, God, I'll be the most careful driver in the whole world. All I want is one more chance. Please, God, I'm only seventeen.

~ John Berrio

III

ATTITUDE

Attitude--more than anything else will determine your success or failure.

Attitudes are either POSITIVE or NEGATIVE-- it's that simple. What is not that simple is what goes into developing them.

The Choice

So many of the problems that plague society today—drug abuse, alcohol abuse, depression, child abuse, spouse abuse, antisocial behavior, and all crime in general—can be reduced to one common denominator: lack of self-esteem and self-concept.

People simply do not like themselves or believe in themselves anymore. We have been brought up in a negative society. Pick up today's newspaper and just scan the headlines. It won't take you long to realize that the news you read, watch, and listen to comes from a negative position.

Each day when your feet hit the floor in the morning, you are faced with a choice. . . "Am I going to give everything I've got to make this a positive day or will I allow negative influences to pull me down so that I'll be like everyone else? Life was meant to be lived in a positive man-ner. No one can make this choice for you. The mental aspect of life is more important than your physical presence. All we are and all we have the potential to become are nothing more than thought.

Richard Bach, in his book *Jonathan Livingston Seagull*, put on paper one of the most powerful thoughts ever written: "YOU MUST BEGIN BY KNOWING YOU HAVE ALREADY ARRIVED."

Then Choose

John is the kind of guy you love to hate. He is always in a good mood and always has something positive to say. When someone would ask him how he was doing, he would reply, "If I were any better, I would be twins!"

He was a natural motivator. If an employee was having a bad day, John was there telling the employee how to look on the positive side on the situation. Seeing his style really made me curious, so one day I went up and asked him, "I don't get it! You can't be a positive person all of the time. How do you do it?"

He replied, "Each morning I wake up and say to myself, you have two choices today. You can choose to be in a good mood. . . or you can choose to be in a bad mood. I choose to be in a good mood!

Each time something bad happens, I can choose to be a victim or I can choose to learn from it. I choose to learn from it. Every time someone comes to me complaining, I can choose to accept their complaining or I can point out the positive side of life. I choose the positive side of life.

"Yeah, right, it's not that easy," I protested.

"Yes, it is," he said. "Life is all about choices. When you cut away all the junk, every situation is a choice. You choose how you react to situations. You choose how people affect your mood. You choose to be in a good mood or bad mood. The bottom line: it's your choice how you live your life."

I reflected on what he said. Soon thereafter, I left my position in the communications tower industry to start my own business. I lost touch with John, but I often thought about him when I made a choice about life instead of reacting to it.

Several years later, I heard that he was involved in a serious accident, falling some 60 feet from a communications tower. After eighteen hours of surgery and weeks of intensive care, he was released from the hospital with rods placed in his back. I saw him about six months after the accident.

When I asked him how he was, he replied, "If I were any better, I'd be twins—Wanna see my scars?" I declined to see his wounds, but I did ask him what had gone through his mind as the accident took place. "The first thing that went through my mind was the well-being of my soon-to-be born daughter," he replied. "Then, as I lay on the ground, I remembered that I had two choices: I could choose to live. . . or I could choose to die. I chose to live."

"Weren't you scared? Did you lose consciousness?" I asked.

He continued, "The paramedics were great. They kept telling me I was going to be fine. But when they wheeled me into the emergency room and I saw the expressions on the faces of the doctors and nurses, I got really scared. In their eyes, I read, 'he's a dead man.' I knew I needed to take action."

"What did you do?" I asked.

"Well, there was a big burly nurse shouting questions at me," said John. She asked if I was allergic to anything. "Yes," I replied. The doctors and nurses stopped working as they waited for me to tell them what I was allergic to. I took a deep breath and yelled, "Gravity!"

Over their laughter, I told them, "I am choosing to live. Operate on me as if I am alive, not dead."

He lived, thanks to the skill of his doctors, but also because of his amazing attitude. . . I learned from him that every day we have the choice to live fully. Attitude, after all, is everything!

Therefore, do not worry about tomorrow, for tomorrow will worry about itself. Each day has enough trouble of its own.
~ Matthew 6:34

After all, today is the tomorrow you worried about yesterday.
~ Unknown

Attitude

The longer I live, the more I realize the impact of attitude on life. Attitude, to me, is more important than education, than money, than circumstances, than failures, than success, than what other people think or say or do. It is more important than appearance, giftedness, or skill. It will make or break a company. . . a church. . . a home. The remark-able thing is we have a choice everyday regarding the attitude we embrace for that day. We cannot change our past. . . we cannot change the fact that people act in a certain way. We cannot change the inevitable. The only thing we can do is play on the one string we have, and that is our attitude. . . I am convinced that life is 10% what happens to me and 90% of how I react to it. And so it is with you. . . we are in charge of our ATTITUDES.

"Your past is history. Your future is a mystery. The present is a gift.
Live each day as if it is your last because one day you'll be right."
~ Chuck Swindoll

Attitude is Everything

Attitude is the way you think. Your attitude is something other people can actually see. They can hear it in your voice, see it in the way you move, feel it when they are with you. Your attitude expresses itself in everything you do, all the time, wherever you are.

Positive attitudes always invite positive results. Negative attitudes always invite negative results.

Attitude makes a difference every hour, every day, in everything that you do for your entire life. What you get out of each thing you do will equal the attitude you have when you do it.

Anything you do with a positive attitude will work for you.

Anything you do with a negative attitude will work against you.

If you have a positive attitude, you are looking for ways to solve problems that you can solve, and you are letting go of things over which you have no control.

You can develop a positive attitude by emphasizing the good, being tough-minded, and by refusing defeat.

The Influence of Attitude

Change your input to change your attitude. If you seek a positive mind, you must expose yourself to positive thinking. You must expose yourself to positive information and associate with positive people. If you want to achieve a positive attitude you have to live it.

1. You were born to win, but you must plan to win, prepare to win, then you can expect to win. ~ Vince Lombardi
2. The will to win is nothing without the desire to prepare for victory. ~ Vince Lombardi
3. You will get whatever you want if you help enough people get whatever they want. (A statement many claim to have said, but it doesn't matter who said it, just live it.)

4. Make every day as productive as the day before you go on vacation. That's a day that everything gets done.
5. Ignore people who tell you "you can't" (except your boss). People will try to rain on your parade because they have no parade of their own.
6. Don't dwell on (whine about) the problem; concentrate on the solution. Resolve how you can, not lament why you can't.
7. Forgive and go forward. Grudges block positive thought. Until you clear the past you are destined to repeat it.
8. Self-talk equals self-performance. Look at athletes—self-talk is a crucial part of their expected positive performance.
9. What is the picture you have of yourself? That is what you will become. Spend 15-minutes a day focusing on your positive picture.
10. You will hear the word "no" 116,000 times in your lifetime. Try converting just 1,000 of them to a "yes" and the world is your oyster.
11. What you do off the job determines what you are likely to do on the job.
12. Strengthen your weaknesses and strengthen your strengths at the same time. Combine positive with negative for better personal development results.
13. Failure is an event, not a person. Think of failure as "it", not "me."
14. It's not what happens to you; it's what you do with what happens to you. Attitude manifests itself in your RESPONSE to events.
15. Every obstacle presents an opportunity if you're looking for it. "Revel" and "lament" are choices.
16. Hard work makes luck. Nothing affects positive circumstances and results more than hard work.
17. How many of your problems are cured with $10,000? My dad once asked me that question as I lamented my problems. If money makes your problem go away, attitude makes them go away as well.
18. It's not what you say; it's how you say it. The tone of your verbiage determines the atmosphere of your environment.
19. Resign your position as general manager of the universe. Don't try to solve other people's problems, until you are problem-free.

And then there are the "Attitude 'Ahas'." Many (many) years ago, I was riding down the road listening to a tape by Earl Nightingale, one of the founding fathers of personal development. The topic was enthusiasm.

"Enthusiasm," Earl said, "comes from the Greek 'ethos,' meaning 'the god within'." Aha! All of a sudden all the other quotes and advice made sense. The strength of self-belief is within your own spirit, if you hunger for the feeling.

Character

"The Discipline of Desire is the Background of Character"

Character is what you're made of on the inside. It's guts. It's what determines your attitude. It is the difference between grace under pressure and choking under pressure. Character is sportsmanship. Character is focus. Character is destiny!

People talk about others' weaknesses in terms of their "character flaws" and their strengths in terms of "character traits." Those with "strong character" tend to challenge themselves to succeed when faced with an obstacle, while someone with "weak character" will fold up his or her tent and quit.

Fourth and goal, or down by two with time for one last shot at the basket; or facing the team across the net serving for match point. Character defines how we act and react in these situations.

The key to developing strong character is having a set of values or rules by which to live and sticking to them. This means hard choices. Whether it's staying after practice to work on your weakness, or to help a teammate work on his or hers, character does whatever it takes without complaining. And every time you make the difficult choices, you exercise your character and make it stronger.

~ John Locke

"Character is destiny."
~ Heraclitus

The Essence of Character

"Your true character is revealed by the clarity of your convictions,
the choices you make, and the promises you keep.
What you say and do defines who you are,
And who you are. . . you are forever."

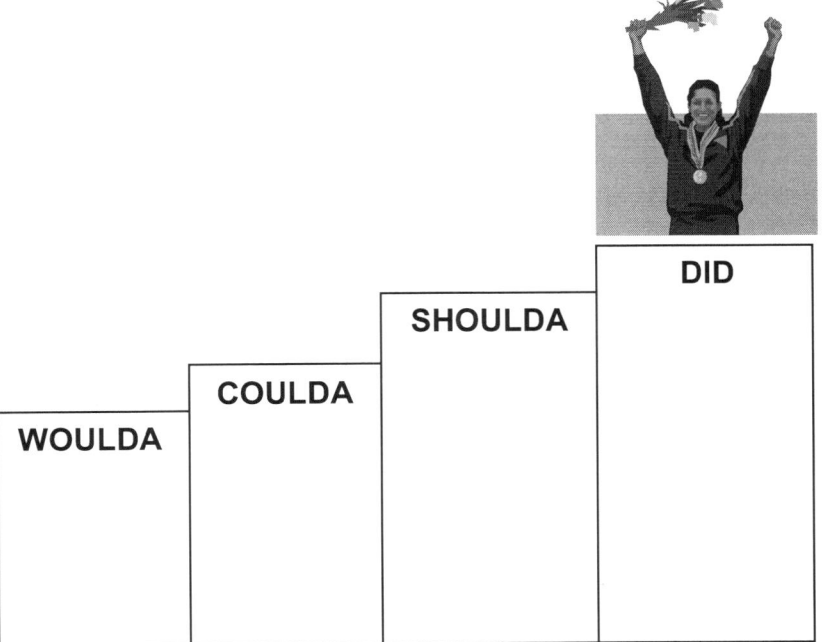

Where will you be standing?
The great thing is, you have the power to make the choice.

Your Attitude will Determine Your Altitude

One of the things that impress most of us as we grow older is how many nice people there are in this world. Even people we used to find annoying or downright irritating don't seem to bother us so much. We discover that many of the ones we didn't particularly like really aren't as bad as we thought.

Maybe you and I are a little smarter than we used to be. We have begun to understand why prickly pears are prickly, and make allowance for it. Other people appreciate the change in the way we react to them, and it makes them friendlier toward us.

Taking this attitude, we have found, makes for smoother sailing. Life becomes friendlier and more enjoyable. You learn to forgive and forget. Those who don't learn this miss out on the warmth and friend-ships they might enjoy.

A passenger traveling on a train from Boston to New York entered the diner and asked for plum pudding for dessert. When told they had no plum pudding, the traveler got very angry. "Do you realize you're talking to one of the biggest shippers over this railroad?" he shouted at the waiter.

By this time the steward came up and assured the man he would try to get some plum pudding when the train stopped at New Haven. True to his promise, as the train left New Haven, the steward came up with plum pudding for the irate diner.

The man looked at it for a moment then pushed it away and threw down his napkin. "To hell with it!" he snorted. "I'd rather be mad at the railroad."

No matter how well things go for some people, no matter how well their companies treat them and provide opportunities for them, they'd rather "be mad." This is unfortunate, because staying mad at the world — and taking it out on one's company or fellow employees—is a sure way to make matters worse.

The people who get on in the world are those who have a positive attitude. They're cooperative, friendly, and fair. They don't knock the company, their bosses, or their fellow workers. They are positive, out-going, and constructive. And they can't lose. People like them, bosses want them, and companies need them.

❖

Success is More Attitude than Aptitude

Your talent determines what you can do. Your motivation determines how much you are willing to do. Your attitude determines how well you will do it.

❖

If someone says you can't accomplish something, it is only an opinion and nothing more. It only becomes a fact when you tell yourself you can't do it.

❖

Commitment, loyalty, attitude, passion, desire. . . Things you can't fake.

❖

Attitude has the power to change your life. Surround yourself with positive people. Do not associate with negative people. Encourage rather than discourage.

❖

Every day, ordinary people do extraordinary things. Today, it's your turn.

❖

Winners and losers aren't born; they are simply products of how they think.

The best and most beautiful things in the world cannot be seen or even touched. They must be felt with the heart.

~ Helen Keller

Dwight D. Eisenhower had a way to avoid carrying a grudge against anyone. "If a man had been guilty of despicable actions, especially toward me, I would try to forgive him," said Eisenhower. "I would write his name down on a piece of scrap paper, drop it into the lowest drawer of my desk, and say to myself, "That finishes the incident and so far as I'm concerned, that drawer became a sort of private wastebasket for discarded personalities. Besides, it seemed to be effective and helped me avoid harboring useless, black feelings."

A psychologist once asked a group of college students to jot down the initials of the people they disliked. Some of the students taking the test could think of only one person. Others listed as many as fourteen.

But the interesting fact that came out of this bit of research was this: Those who disliked the largest number of people were themselves the most widely disliked.

❖

Of all the things you wear, your expression is the most important.

❖

How much we enjoy what we have is more important than how much we have. Life is full of people who have more than they know what to do with, but cannot be content. It is the capacity to enjoy life that brings contentment.

❖

There are two ways you can get others to do what you want: compulsion or persuasion. Persuasion is the method of free people.

To persuade requires an understanding of how people tick, of what motivates them—knowledge of human nature.

In a recent poll, seventy psychologists were asked, "What is the most essential thing for a supervisor to know about human nature?" Two-thirds said that knowing how to motivate people is the most powerful tool in dealing with them.

❖

When the other fellow acts that way, he's ugly. When you do it, it is nerves.

When he's set in his ways, he's obstinate. When you are, it is just firmness.

When he doesn't like your friends, he's prejudiced. When you don't like his, you are simply showing good judgment of human nature.

When he tries to be accommodating, he's polishing the apple. When you do it, you're using tact.

When he takes time to do things, he is dead slow. When you take ages, you are deliberate.

When he picks at flaws, he's cranky. When you do it, you're discriminating.

Success Comes from Self-Satisfaction
in Knowing You Gave the Best
You are Capable of!

~ John Wooden

| **AMBITION** **CONCENTRATION** **DETERMINATION** **FIGHT** | COMPETITIVE GREATNESS Real love of a battle. Be at your best when your best is needed. | **RELIABILITY** **INTEGRITY** **HONESTY** **SINCERITY** |

| POISE Just being yourself. At ease in any situation. Never fighting yourself. | CONFIDENCE Respect without fear. Confidence without cockiness. Faith in yourself. |

| CONDITION Mental, moral & physic-al. Practice moderation, no dissipation. Consider rest, exercise & diet. | SKILL Proper execution of fundamentals. No substitution for "knowing your stuff." Be prepared. | TEAM SPIRIT The team comes first. Sacrifice personal glory for the welfare of the team. |

| SELF-CONTROL Delicate adjustment between mind & body. Emotions under control. | ALERTNESS Alive & observing constantly. Quick to see an opening & quicker to utilize it. | INITIATIVE Leadership qualities. Ability to think alone. Desire to be in front. | INTENTNESS Resist temptation & stay with your course. Concentrate on your purpose. |

| INDUSTRIOUS-NESS No substitute for work. Seek perfection by practice. Never be satisfied. | FRIENDSHIP Comes from mutual esteem. Respect & devotion. Sincere liking for all | LOYALTY To yourself & all who are depending upon you. Keep your self-respect. | COOPERATION Losing yourself in the group for the good of the group. Help in every way. | ENTHUSIASM Your heart must be in your work. Stimulate others. |

Wanted — a Man

A man. . . who can find things to be done without the help of a manager and three assistants.

A man. . . who gets to work on time in the morning and does not imperil the lives of others in an attempt to be the first to quit work at night.

A man. . . who listens carefully when he is spoken to and asks only enough questions to insure the accurate carrying out of instructions.

A man. . . who looks you straight in the eye and tells the truth every time.

A man. . . who does not pity himself for having to work.

A man. . . who is cheerful, courteous to everyone, and always determined to "make good."

A man. . . who, when he does not know, says, "I don't know," and when he is asked to do anything says, "I'll try."

~ Toledo Rotary Spoke

Loyalty

If, you work for a man, in heaven's name, work *for* him; speak well of him and stand by the institution he represents. Remember, an ounce of loyalty is worth a pound of cleverness. If you must growl, condemn, and eternally find fault, resign your position; and when you are on the outside, damn to your heart's content, but as long as you are a part of the institution, do not condemn it. If you do, the first high wind that comes along will blow you away, and probably you will never know why.

~ Elbert Hubbard

❖

It's a fact—
No two people looking
at the same thing at the
same time

EVER SEE EXACTLY
THE SAME THING!

WHY?

Because what they "see" depends on their
purposes and their experiences.

Winners versus Losers

The Winner is always part of the answer;
The Loser is always part of the problem.

The Winner always has a program;
The Loser always has an excuse.

The Winner says, "Let me do it for you;"
The Loser says; "That is not my job."

The Winner sees an answer for every problem;

The Loser sees a problem for every answer.

The Winner says, "It may be difficult but it is possible;"
The Loser says, "It may be possible but it is too difficult."

When a Winner makes a mistake, he says, "I was wrong;"
When a Loser makes a mistake, he says, "It wasn't my fault."

A Winner makes commitments;
A Loser makes promises.

Winners have dreams;
Losers have schemes.

Winners say, "I must do something;"
Losers say, "Something must be done."

Winners are a part of the team;
Losers are apart from the team.

Winners see the gain;
Losers see the pain.

Winners see possibilities;
Losers see problems.
Winners see the potential;
Losers see the past.

Winners are like a thermostat;
Losers are like thermometers.

Winners choose what they say;
Losers say what they choose.

Winners use hard arguments but soft words;
Losers use soft arguments but hard words.

Winners stand firm on values but compromise on petty things;

Losers stand firm on petty things but compromise on values.

Winners follow the philosophy of empathy,
"Don't do to others what you would not want them to do to you;"
Losers follow the philosophy,
"Do it to others before they do it to you."

Winners make it happen;
Losers let it happen.

The Locker Room

The mind of an athlete is a powerful weapon. My weapon begins working each time I step into the locker room, a special room, my room, where my pregame rituals always remain the same. It is in this room where I first take seat on the bench, when I mentally begin preparing myself for the game.

I begin with a thought process which tells me there are two kinds of athletes in this world: athletes who set goals and meet them and athletes who set goals but never act on them. Myself, I am an athlete, born and raised. I act on the goals I set for myself!

As I begin to undress the layer of life which matters no more, I remind myself how lucky I really am. How lucky I am to have my health! How lucky I am to have been given these abilities to play this game that I love so much! Most of all though, is how lucky I am to dress myself with pride in this uniform once again.

As I lace up my shoes and look around the room, I pray that my teammates have similar thoughts. I pray that they understand the significance of this room; that this is our meeting place. It is the place where we have shared so many good times, but also helped one another get through the bad, the place where we have come together again to prepare ourselves for another fight of our lives. I have now fine-tuned my weapon, and I am ready to make my goals become reality. I am ready to go out there and play this game as if it were the last game I was ever able to play. I reflect upon one final thought: how thankful I am for the opportunity to once again enter and leave "the locker room."

IV

THE ATHLETES' CREED

Concentration

Heart

Attitude

Modesty

Practice

Sacrifice

Every Victory is Won Before the Game Is Played:
The Power Of Attitude

Mental Condition

The mental condition of a team is of far more importance than the ability to execute basic physical techniques.

❖

If a player has a genuine desire to win, he will exert himself to the maximum, both in practice and in games.

❖

If a player has an unselfish attitude, he will be far more interested in the good of the team rather than personal glory.

❖

If a player has confidence, he can perform at his best in the pressure situation.

❖

If a player is receptive to criticism, his rate of improvement will be increased.

❖

We must have the right mental attitude if we are to be successful. This means that we must have great team morale. Teams with tremendous potential have faltered for lack of it. Remember—you don't put morale on like a coat—you build it day by day. START DOING YOUR PART NOW.

Because of the great importance of the proper mental attitude, the mental approach to the game has been placed at the beginning of this section. Please do not take this part lightly. We cannot succeed physically unless we can mentally. Study this section as you would any part of this book.

❖

Athletics

To Play:

1. Be Committed to Work Hard — Programs are built on the concept that hard work pays off. We believe that we work harder than anyone else. . . and because of that we always deserve to win. There is a reason we are the best. We work at it.
2. Be Committed to Becoming a Smart Player — Players must be ready to learn. We believe that we work smarter than anyone else. We must develop players to understand the game. Players must be good listeners and learn by watching. We must make good decisions and we must play with poise. We prepare mentally for practice and games.
3. Commit Yourself to a Winning Attitude — Players must be committed to winning but understand we do not measure our success by winning alone. Each time we play we evaluate ourselves on reaching our potential. The test for our team is to play against the game, not just the opponent. We never quit. . . we always look for a way to win.

To Win:

1. Believe in Our System — Commit yourself to our philosophy and our system of play. Be a sponge and soak up the concept of how we play. Learn your role. . . then accept it and do it the best you can.
2. Believe in Yourself — Play with confidence. . . think positive . . . realize you are a great player in a great program. Do not get down when you play poorly. Realize you were chosen to be here. Now you are a leader. . . lead by example.
3. Believe In Your Teammates — Communicate with each other. Help each other. Encourage and support each other. Be friends; understand that we are all different. Be tolerant of teammates and others. Remember the strength of the pack is the wolf and the strength of the wolf is the pack.

4. <u>Believe in Your Coaches</u> — Know that your coaches are trying to make you better people and players. Ask questions. Do not whine and complain. Learn to take tough coaching. You must believe that the coaches are doing what they think is right for the team and you.

5. <u>Be Committed to the Program</u> — We realize that our players are in a fish bowl. Every word and action will be watched. Our program's reputation provides many opportunities, yet brings many responsibilities. We must be committed to build onto tradition of our program and respect those that have gone before us and paid the price to build the program.

Champs

Here is an attempt to explain the word "Champs" by breaking it down into its component parts and then defining each letter:

C – Concentration
H – Heart
A – Attitude
M – Modesty
P – Practice
S – Sacrifice

<u>Concentration</u>:

Evidence of concentration is when the coach asks a player to drill <u>once</u> and he does it a <u>hundred</u> times to gain skill adroitness, instead of the coach asking a <u>hundred</u> times in order for the player to do it <u>once</u>.

Concentration means being absorbed, drowned in his work, because of the overwhelming desire to succeed. It includes focusing his entire personality on the project until he is lost. All of his energies, conscious and unconscious, are marshaled for one single purpose—the task at hand.

<u>Heart</u>:

It takes a lot of heart to continue to play a sport in the face of adversity and defeat. Some players are front runners and excel only when they are ahead. The real hallmark of a champion is his ability to come back—to come from behind.

Attitude:

You must possess willingness to practice every day to perfect game skills. It is a manifestation of good player attitude.

Pride must be mentioned as a significant element in attitude. You must take pride in your play. You must hurt when you lose. Anyone who loses and is satisfied can no longer be a member of the team. I want men on the team who take the blame for a defeat and refuse to accept any other reason for failing. I want a hole to burn in you until accounts are squared. No rest can ever be felt by a real contestant who has suffered defeat. I want you to suffer mental anguish when you are outscored.

Modesty:

No matter what success you may achieve in a sport, always be modest. Do not ever think you are the best, because somewhere there is someone better, much better, than you.

Practice:

"Nothing succeeds like success" is a well-known axiom but its corollary, "Nothing fails like failure," carries more impact.

Team

"Team" is one of those popular words coaches like to use and everyone acts as if the meaning of the word is understood. Yet, a team is a complex entity and is envisioned differently among individuals.

To some, a team is simply one person helping another, and that is an acceptable definition. To others, it means a change from personal identity to a collective identity. The second definition of a team, the collective identity concept, provides a glimpse of the power a team yields. The concept of collective identity is what true teams try to achieve and maintain.

Who is on the team? Believe me, there are a lot more members on the team than just the players. The team, at large, also includes the coaching staff, the administration, and the players' parents. All of these folks are part of the team whether you like it or not.

Purpose:

The word 'purpose' implies a sense of direction; a team needs to know why it exists and what its goals are.

Trust:

Once a team has a purpose, all the members need to "buy in" and work towards a common goal. Trust is required from each person to rely on others to do their individual responsibilities.

For players, they need to trust each other to do a hundred things, from showing up on time, staying eligible for play and performance, and playing their roles as designed. Coaches must trust their staff members to do their jobs in the delegating of their tasks. Parents must trust the coaches to operate professionally and stay in control and oversee the roles of all members of the team. In turn, coaches and players must trust that the parents will not hurt the program by interfering, complaining or not cooperating with one another.

Any member that is not responsible dissolves the team trust because undependable people force others to interfere, complain and become uncooperative.

Self-sacrifice:

The true team has a collective identity intent on achieving a common goal. Team members can easily trust one another because they want the same goal. Mistakes are tolerated because they are not made to be purposely detrimental. Individual people just stumble once in a while. To fall is just part of learning. Teammates pick one another up and try to help one another. This teamwork collectively puts people in a natural state where everybody is headed in the same direction.

Does it really happen that way?

A coach can be fooled by the players, their parents and even by the administration. The problem is that everybody gives lip service to the ideals of teamwork, but few are willing to sacrifice anything to achieve it. Sacrifice is essential to building a team. If you think about it, if it doesn't cost anything to make something, is that something worth anything?

A team's worth is measured by the sacrifices made to build it.

How to Kill a Team? Destroy Its Leadership!:

Discrediting the leadership (coaches or captains) is a very common practice by those who wish to hurt the team. If it is possible to generate a loss of confidence in the coach, then it is possible to destroy his ability to apply a direction. A common method (and with the advantage of hindsight) is to second-guess the coach's decisions after the game. Some parents, when dissatisfied with the coach, will actually tell the player, "You don't need to listen to your coach."

By distracting players from directions given by the coach, parents who provide a different coaching method at home going contrary to the coach are detrimental to the players during the game. When this tactic is used by one player and the other team players are unfamiliar with it, it causes confusion and distrust.

Team Spirit

We want no "one-man" players, no "stars." We want a team made up of five boys at a time, each of whom is a forward, a guard, and a center combined; in other words, each boy should be able to score, out-jump or out-smart one opponent, or prevent the opposing team from scoring, as the occasion demands.

No chain is stronger than its weakest link; no team is stronger than its weakest boy. One boy attempting to "grandstand" can wreck the best team ever organized. We must be "one for all and all for one" with every boy giving his very best every second. There is no place for selfishness or egotism on our squad.

We want a squad of fighters afraid of no club, not cocky and not conceited. A team that plays hard, plays fair, but plays to win—always remembering that a "team that won't be beaten, can't be beaten." We want our boys to believe that, "A winner never quits and a quitter never wins." Make up your mind before the game that you won't lose, that you can outsmart and out-fight the opposing team; in other words, if you have confidence in your team's ability to win, you will be plenty tough to whip.

Others may be faster than you are; larger than you are, and have more ability than you have—but no one should ever be your superior in team spirit, fight, determination, ambition, and character.

By far the most important characteristic that we hope to find in our players is competitive spirit. That indomitable spirit that drives on after others have quit, that spirit that is fighting hardest and enjoying it most when the going is toughest is the highest goal of achievement of any competitor. The coach is constantly looking and hoping for that boy who is at his very best when his very best is needed, and not the "front runner" who shines when the going is easy.

What Does it Take to be a Great Player?

Being a basketball player does not imply merely wearing the uniform and being just a member of the squad. There are many more important phases to think about if you want to be a winner not only in a sport, but in life as well. Your coaches want to impress you with the importance of the following qualities absolutely necessary for every great basketball player.

1. Are you Coachable? Can you take coaching? Can you take criticism without ever looking for an alibi? Are you a "know it all?" Will you always do your level best to try to improve?

2. Are you possessed with the spirit of competition, which fires an intense desire to win? Do you want to win with a passion? Does it hurt you to lose? Will you skin your nose and knees going for the loose ball—or is winning not that important?

3. Are you willing to practice? This doesn't mean just reporting and putting in the necessary time but working every day with the same

zeal, speed, and determination you use during a ball game? Do you have two speeds—a practice speed and a game speed? The great basketball player must have one speed and it must be the same every day, every practice, every game. If you loaf and cheat in practice you will loaf and cheat in a ball game.

4. Are you willing to make sacrifices? Conditioning to play demands work; training is exacting; the responsibility is heavy. It is rough and includes personal denials in order to remain in tip-top condition, but it has its rewards. The only way for you to remain in good shape is to never get out of it.

5. Do you have an ardent desire to improve? Are you willing to practice the things you cannot do three times longer that the things you can do? Are you willing to put in long hours, concentrating on a skill until you have perfected it? We have seen too many men spend their time doing what they already do well. They never improved.

6. Do you have the ability to think under fire? Can you concentrate on the work to be accomplished at the moment? Can you shut out from your mind a previous failure, success, rule infraction, or personal insult in order to give undivided attention to the offensive and defensive maneuver in the here and now? Games are not won by yesterday's score, but by what is happening now, at this moment. Great basketball players play every minute up to the hilt—never depending on past success to aid them.

7. Are you willing to be impersonal toward your opponents? Do you shut out all personal feelings about your opponent? Our experiences have taught us that the moment a player be-comes personal he plays only to release individual grievances and ceases to play basketball as a team member.

8. Do you believe in your school, your team, and your coach? Your school is as good as you make it. Your coach is a genuine employee of your school given the responsibility of coaching, not his team, but your team. Are you willing to work toward that spirit of oneness so that everyone possesses the feeling of belonging through their contributions? Will you keep uppermost in mind that when a coach blisters the team with criticism, his remarks are never meant to be personal affronts? The only intent is to pressurize you to want to rectify your omissions so that success for all

results.
9. Are you willing to study just as hard as before coming out for a sport? Sports are never meant to take the place of studies. The athletic tail must never wag the academic dog. This involves re-alignment in your time schedule. If a sport will consume two hours of your day, then you must draw time not from your scholastic program but from hours previously devoted to personal pursuits. If you must eliminate something from your schedule, it must not be study time. First things come first, and your academic growth is of paramount importance.
10. Will you strive daily to improve in every respect? This not only means diligent work to develop skillful techniques. Will you con-stantly strive to improve your mental attitude toward the game, your relationships with your fellow players and coaches? Are you willing to make a daily effort toward improving yourself as a per-son? It will pay off for you—in life and on the field, court or wher-ever you are playing.

Will You Play on a Championship Team?

Basketball is a game that separates the men from the boys. A basket-ball player who does not act like a champion on and off the court will never be one. There is a term used in reference to the real champs. You've heard them referred to as "Real Pros." They go about their business quietly and unassumingly. They don't pout, stamp their feet, screw up their faces, nor hang their heads when they make a mistake and are chastised by the coach. Those who act this way are also given a name, "Bush Leaguer."

A "Real Pro" will exert himself to the best of his ability at all times lest an opponent beat him. The "Real Pro" thinks of his team before himself because his uppermost thoughts are to win. He has learned from experi-ence that he himself will not succeed unless his team succeeds. He would rather be a little dog on a championship team than the "Big Cheese" on an nonentity.

A "Real Pro" is the type of player who constantly tries to improve his game. There are many players with lots of ability who are satisfied to get by without improvements but the "Real Pro" is not satisfied with his play and is constantly trying to improve his game.

When you compete in sports, it is impossible to avoid bumps, bruises, or small injuries. If you are doing a good job, these things are bound to happen. There are certain players on every team who will not do their best when they are not playing well. These boys become a real handicap to their teammates. A "Real Pro" never lessens his efforts for anything less than a major injury.

We want to urge every player to set his goal towards becoming a "Real Pro." We want a championship team. There has never been a championship team that did not have some "Real Pros" playing their hardest at all times, putting the team above self, helping their team-mates, constantly improving their game, ignoring minor injuries and setting a high standard for their teammates to follow. To be a champion, you must live and play like a champion; let's start now!

Be Big Where it Counts

THE FIGHT—IT'S THE SIZE OF THE FIGHT IN THE DOG. . . The size of the player's HEART is much, much more important than his physical size. HEART is a partner of COURAGE and it takes both to excel. WE MUST BE BIG WHERE IT COUNTS.

Confidence:

I have never known a great athlete who didn't have confidence. Think of the good Athletes that you have known, I'm sure you will agree that confidence was one of their characteristics.

Let's not confuse confidence with cockiness or conceit. Cockiness is shouting the belief to the world. We don't want that. We do want to feel that we can match or outplay our opponent in any department. If each of you will believe in yourself, your teammates, and your coach, we will be hard to beat. You have the ability, but you will be no better than you think you are.

Some players have difficulty understanding criticism and lose confidence when criticized. Others understand that criticism is a sign of interest by the coach.

Condition:

Conditioning is strenuous in all sports. Sports demand a great deal of endurance. Every player is expected in top physical condition. Sports demand a great deal of endurance to be able to go at top speed. Let's make sure that our physical condition is superior to our opponents.

Good training demands self-discipline, and this is not beyond any player who wants to make the squad. During the season you must be willing to sacrifice and deny yourself many things other students enjoy. This is a matter of will power. Training, however, is actually no more than good common sense habits. Remember, you must set the example for younger athletes. An intelligent and dedicated athlete will stay in shape. Alcohol and tobacco have no place in winning sports.

The three most important factors in training are exercise, sleep, and eating. Your practices will be designed to give the proper amount of work. Regularity in eating and sleeping is up to you. At least eight hours of sleep is required and eating three well-balanced meals is necessary. Regularity in your habits is extremely important. Let's start getting into shape now.

Cooperation:

All team sports require a lot of player cooperation. Players must always stand together as a unit and our team sprit and morale depends upon a "one for all and all for one" attitude. If you are a good player, it is because your teammates have a lot to do with it. A great player is one without jealousies. Its players do their jobs well, get along together, respect each other, and cooperate.

If you will avoid passing judgment on one another we will have a happy team. Griping, razzing, and criticizing do nothing but cause hard feelings. I reserve for myself the right to coach the team and make the criticisms.

We will all be living and traveling together for the next few months. Let's cooperate to make it a successful season.

Coaching:

The success of my coaching will depend a lot upon the reception you give it. You can be sure that there will be a great deal of experience, thought, and organization behind every practice and game. Our progress will be determined by your capacity to learn and improve. You will like our style of play, and certainly it has proven to be a winning style of play.

Every player will be given an equal opportunity to start, but it must be realized that final judgment on all matters rests with me. This is a brand-new season and that means a fresh start for all.

All of the coaches will give their very best to make this a good season. In return, much will be expected of you in the way of loyalty, respect, and conformity to our wishes and rules. No matter how experienced the captain of the ship may be, he cannot safely guide it into port unless he has loyalty and respect for his coach and teammates.

If you are faced with personal problems, I want you to feel free to come to me for help and advice. As long as you are doing your part, I'll go to bat for you and help you in every possible way.

An Atmosphere of Greatness

We are inclined to accept the thesis that sport is all physicality, and that athletes are all muscle and bone. However, I am going to prove a different hypothesis. The world of sports is more determined by thought and goals than anything else. The world of sports is a world of emotion; it's a world of temper and most of all it's a world of ideas.

The French believe that every great man that has ever lived has a fixed concept, idée fixe, of what he wants to be. They believe that this fixed goal is the vital determination of life. I have been in sports for over twenty-five years and would like to give you three shocking summaries.

1. Great athletes will tell you that they're going to do it.
2. They predict to a tenth of a second the races that they are going to run or swim.
3. In most cases it is thought to be impossible. It has not before been done in the history of the world.

They have an "idée fixe", a mental process of what they're going to do in life. Billie Jean King, Peggy Fleming, Johnny Bench, Mark Spitz are all examples of athletes that have predicted their success. I have watched this in athlete after athlete. They tell you what they're going to do long before they do it.

You become like the "idea fixed" in your brain. You become like the thing you go for. That's why I say set out to be the greatest. In whatever profession you go into, go out to be the best in the world; because you will become like the things you go after. The great ones go for the impossible. They go for world records.

You are what you think. The capacity of a person is still unknown. Muscles are capable of 100 times more work than the built-in-limiter, the brain, will permit. Every weight lifter will tell you that you must think you can lift the weight before your body can. It is staggering to realize in this world of so-called "muscle and bone," the mind is the determining factor.

Psychologists who study great people in all walks of life in an attempt to find a common denominator for greatness cannot agree on anything except a principle called "F.Q." or Failure Quotient. F.Q. is the ability to bounce back. The great ones can be beaten but they bounce back. They do not let an injury or a mistake beat them. You will not be great unless you have a high F.Q. along with an "Idée Fixe." You have to be beaten and have the ability to bounce back to be great.

You are what you think. Expect a miracle and it will happen. You are programmed for success. All of us are over-endowed. We have capabilities that we haven't scratched the surface of yet. We have physical powers that we haven't even discovered. We are made to win; and it takes a lot of messing up and wrong thinking to keep you from triumphing in life. Learning any sport and knowing you can win is part of this great game called "living."

~ Reverend Bob Richards

IT"S ALL IN THE STATE OF MIND

WINNERS AND LOSERES AREN'T BORN:
THEY ARE SIMPLY PRODUCTS OF HOW THEY THINK. . .
ATTITUDE

What it Takes to be No. 1
"You've Got to Pay the Price"

"Winning is not a sometime thing. It's an all the time thing. You don't win once in a while; you don't do things right once in a while; you do them right all the time. Winning is a habit. Unfortunately, so is losing.

There is no room for second place. There is only one place in my game and that is first place. I have finished second twice in my time at Green Bay and I don't ever want to finish second again. There is a second place bowl game, but it is a game for losers played by losers. It is and always has been an American zeal to be first in anything we do and to win and to win and to win.

Every time a football player goes out to play his trade, he's got to play from the ground up, from the soles of his feet right up to his head. Every inch of him has to play. Some guys play with their heads. That's okay. You've got to be smart to be No. 1 in any business. But more importantly, you've got to play with your heart—with every fiber of your body. If you're lucky enough to find a guy with a lot of head and a lot of heart, he's never going to come off the field second.

Running a football team is no different from running any other kind of organization, any army, a political party, a business. The principles are the same. The object is to win—to beat the other guy. Maybe that sounds hard or cruel. I don't think it is.

It is a reality of life that men are competitive and the most competitive games draw the most competitive men. That's why they're there—to compete. They know the rules and the objectives when they get in the game. The objective is to win—fairly, squarely, decently, by the rules, but to win.

In truth, I've never known a man worth his salt who, in the long run, deep down in his heart, didn't appreciate the grind, the discipline. There is something in good men that really yearns for deeds, discipline, and the harsh reality of head-to-head combat.

I don't say these things because I believe in the "brute" nature of man or that men must be brutalized to be combative. I believe in God, and I believe in human decency. But I firmly believe that any man's finest hour—his greatest fulfillment to all he holds dear—is that moment when he has worked his heart out in a good cause and lies exhausted on the field of battle—victorious."   ~ Vince Lombardi

"Choking" in Sports: It's All in the Mind

The dirtiest word in sports has five letters. An athlete can do nothing worse than "<u>choke</u>."

Choking is a concept that intrigued Lou Pelliccioni from the day he started coaching basketball. What can be done, he wondered, about the kid who can stuff the ball backward in practice, but can't dribble when the game begins?

After 10 years, Pelliccioni, West Virginia assistant basketball coach and candidate for a doctorate in sports psychology, thinks he's found some of the answers.

With Michael D. Scott, a communications professor, Pelliccioni has written, *Don't Choke: How Athletes Can Become Winners,* a paperback published by Prentice-Hall.

While working on his master's degree in speech communications, Pelliccioni learned that the No. 1 fear in America is to give a public speech. Choking, he decided, is the athlete's form of stage fright. After all, walking up to the foul line in a gym full of people is at least as terrifying as stepping to a microphone in a room full of people.

If we can teach people to overcome stage fright, why can't we teach athletes to overcome choking? If an athlete has the physical talent to shoot in practice, there's no reason he can't do it in a game.

"We teach the physical side of athletics so much," Pelliccioni said, "but we only give lip service to the mental side. In many ways, the mental side of sports is as important as the physical side."

"An athlete mentally ready for a game clears his mind of negative thoughts," Pelliccioni said, "because mental tension can lead to muscular tension. A lot of people see themselves missing a shot, thus prompting them to miss."

Pelliccioni continued, "Some athletes put a lot of pressure on themselves, thinking about what the game means to the team and the fans. If they do that, they are not going to be loose and free. The mind can't tell the difference between what is real and what isn't. If you think there is a lot of pressure on you, there will be."

Pelliccioni said to "replace negative thoughts with something positive, blocking out all distractions such as crowd noise at the same time. A golfer could just repeat to himself something simple, like, 'the swing is the thing,' or even something inane like 'alley oop'.

"It should be practiced every day. If you don't do it every day, you won't do it in pressure situations. When you are anxious, you forget new learning," said Pelliccioni, who has worked with basketball players, baseball players and golfers. He said there are six areas an athlete needs to work on: 1) relaxation, 2) concentration, 3) thinking patterns, 4) self-statements, 5) rational attitudes, and 6) proper playing strategy.

By rational attitudes, Pelliccioni means a player must realize he's not going to sink every shot or hit a home run every time up.

"Everybody talks about what a good basketball player Jerry West was here at West Virginia," Pelliccioni said, "but he missed a lot of shots, too. West missed some shots that would have won games, yet he was known as a great clutch player.

"Just because you missed a shot doesn't mean you choked," Pelliccioni said. "People miss shots all the time."

~ *Pressure is Self-Inflicting!*—Dan Donovan

One Possession

It was only one possession,
Why must my coach scream?
My poor defense permitted the basket,
But what can one hoop mean?

As the pass comes my direction,
And I fumble it into the stands,
The coach's voice rings loud and clear,
"Catch with your eyes and hands!"

C'mon coach; it's a single possession,
Our team will be okay,
It's just the first two minutes,
My gosh, we got all day.

At the second quarter mark I remember,
That the center is strong and stout,
A put back for two, quite simply due
To my failure to turn and block out.

But it was only one possession,
I didn't commit a crime,
My team is ahead and I'm playing well,
And there's still plenty of time!

As the halftime buzzer is sounding,
And I watch the ball bank in,
I know I will hear from my loving coach,
Of my questionable effort to defend.

But it was only one possession,
Coach – don't have a heart attack!
We're down by one, but we are having fun,
I know we'll get the lead back!

The second half mirrors the first,
But it's early; it's not a big deal.
That my failure to use a pass fake,
Results in an unlikely steal.

But I quickly I sing a jumper,
I'm greeted by high fives and slaps,
But the next possession I give up a lay-up,
While suffering a mental lapse.
But it's only one possession.
C'mon coach, chill out.
It's crazy to see you disgusted,
As you slap the assistant and shout.

"Victory favors the team making the fewest mistakes.
Single possessions are the key.
So treat them like gold and do as you are told.

And play with intensity."

I step to the line for one and one,
But I'm having a concentration lapse.
The ball soars through the air – Good Lord, it's a brick!
I'm afraid the support will collapse.

In post-game I sit at my locker,
Pondering what more I could do.
I realize the value of each possession,
What a shame that we lost by two.

~ contributed by Coach Paul McNeal, Bunkie, LA

The Right Attitude

At age seven, Chris Seilkop was like every other boy. After his right foot was mangled in a lawn mower accident, it was sports that proved that he still was.

Chris woke up one day to find that his right leg now ended in a stump below his knee. Sympathy was readily available, but Chris wasn't looking for excuses—he just wanted to play ball.

It was this focus and commitment that led Chris to become an accomplished athlete, leading him from stand-out high school basketball player to one of the world's best volleyball middle blockers.

As the youngest of six, competing was second nature to Chris. His peewee football coach called him courageous. Chris just wanted to play.

His first prosthesis was basically a block of wood shaped like his lower leg. It irritated his skin after two hours, causing bleeding and swelling. But the only way his coach would know was if he caught the slight limp that betrayed the pain. And while a wooden leg may have prevented him from going past junior high in football, his 6'6" frame was welcomed on the basketball court.

The intensity of his play resulted in several "broken legs." And despite humiliations like taking the court with his "foot" turned backwards, he never let his injury interfere with his game. He even learned to turn it while hopping to the dressing room at half-time. Once, with his team whittled down to six players, he leisurely adjusted his prosthetic leg to give his teammates a much needed breather.

After high school, Chris was frustrated by the lack of competitive sporting opportunities for a disabled player—a term for which he had little use. After investigating several opportunities he learned that disabled basketball competition was relegated to wheelchair play, so he looked into volleyball. What he found was a sport with enormous potential but badly in need of an infusion of competitive spirit. Chris was the man for the job.

After a shaky two years with the team, including a meltdown in the bronze medal match at the Atlanta Para-Olympics, the U.S. Disabled volleyball team has been posting an impressive record, including gold in the recent Pan American games in Toronto.

The team is made up of athletes with various disabilities ranging from birth defects to cancer. The dynamic of the team has now been worked out. They've settled into their roles, the attitude is right and the vision is understood by all. They are now ranked number two in the world.

Chris, 28, sees some milestones ahead for the U.S. team with international challenges in Poland and Australia. In the meantime, Chris and the team are staying sharp playing able-bodied teams, making no excuses and winning. To this team, overcoming challenges is just part of the game.

Work

So, practice makes perfect. Or does it? Think about this one. If you practice by simply going through the motions, not concentrating on the task at hand, can you really expect to go into a game and perform perfectly when it counts? The answer is no.

So it's actually *perfect* practice that makes perfect. And perfect practice equals hard work.

Some people believe that talent is God-given. That is, it is written into our genetic codes that we will be, for example, a great basketball, volleyball, or football player. And while it is true that some people's bodies might develop to be naturally taller, bigger or faster, it's blood, sweat and tears that makes champions, regardless of your genetic makeup.

If you've ever won anything, chances are you worked pretty hard for it. Think about the moment in your life when you were the most proud of yourself. Was it when you looked at the grade on your final exam and saw a big, fat "A"? Was it when you held your first championship trophy in your hand? Whatever the case, part of the reason you felt such pride was because you worked hard for what you got. You put in the time. But behind that pride was something even more important—the fact that the work you put in also strengthened your character beyond measure.

Some Quotes about Work:

"I've always believed that if you put in the work, the results will come."
~ Michael Jordan

"I find I'm luckier when I work harder."
~ Dr. Denton Cooley

"If a task is once begun, never leave it 'til it's done. Be the labor great or small, do it well, or not at all."
~ Unknown

Sacrifice

Your life is a series of choices and consequences. Once you make the decision to be great, you must accept the sacrifices greatness demands.

Giving something up is never easy. But in order to reach your ultimate potential, you'll have to. There's no getting around it. It's the price you pay. The more you're willing to give up in order to focus on your dreams, the more likely you are to achieve them.

In 1972, at the city basketball championship in a small Midwestern town, Thomas Jefferson High found itself down by two points with enough time left for one last shot. The coach called his team over to the bench. One player, Lewis Tippet, calmly assured his teammates and his coach that if he was given the ball, he would make the shot. He got his chance.

The inbound pass was made and Tippet got the ball just beyond half court. With one dribble, he calmly eyed up his shot, and then he took it.

With the clock showing double zeros, the ball passed through the net without touching the rim, sending the game into overtime. The team and the fans went wild. The spark Lewis Tippet provided ignited the team, and they won in overtime 63-58.

After the game a local newspaper reporter asked Tippet what he thought of his amazing shot. Tippet replied that he never had any doubt he would make it. And when the reporter asked how he could've been so sure, Tippet simply said, "I knew I would make it because I had to. I'd given up way too much to come this far and miss."

Lewis Tippet taught his team, and the world, a valuable lesson that day: the sacrifices we make can actually inspire us to greatness.

Some Quotes about Sacrifice:

"Winning isn't everything. To win is."

~ Catfish Hunter

"Mr. Meant-to has a comrade, and his name is Didn't do; have you ever chanced to meet them? Did they ever call on you? These two fellows live together in the house of Never-win. And I'm told that it is haunted by the ghost of Might-have-been."

~ Unknown

"You get what you pay for."   ~ Unknown

A Coach's Words:
Get on the Line

There are many different types of lines in sports: court lines, field lines, headlines, red and blue lines, box score lines, and finish lines. There are lines that people feed you, sometimes encouraging, some-times degrading. Then there is the line that I implore them to "get on." And there is never a question of what line I mean.

For the athlete, there is something universal, scary, invigorating, and nostalgic about getting on the line, because though the line invites pain, from it, everything is possible. I tell them the line is the beginning of a journey—to potential greatness. I understand the athletes' hunger, and my duty is to feed them. I refuse to press start on my stopwatch until all feet are on the line, and as one, they eventually learn hot to embrace it. They will reach every line in pain, faces taut, thighs burning, emotions giving way to fatigue, and then hardening into will; inevitable contempt transformed into drive channeled into a goal. And though they feel the anxious stomach pains every time they ponder the physical anguish associated with the line, I know that someday they will recognize the fine line between fear and commitment. They will come together in emotion associated with a common struggle for excellence that they wish would come easily but that I know does not. They will endure now in athletics and succeed later in the game of life because they willingly challenged themselves each time they stepped up to the line.

Today, my players run because I tell them to, but tomorrow they will understand it was all for them, and will never forget a coach's words: "Get on the line!"

Return to Heaven

"As I cross over the line from the outside world and set foot onto the hardwood of a basketball court, I transcend into a being that words cannot describe. No longer do I concern myself with worldly problems. Now I am in my domain, my heaven here on earth. With each stride that I take and every creak I hear in the floor, I embrace punishment, fearing someone else may be working harder than me. I notice the smell of pride in the air, and this excites me.

The blood, sweat and tears from the agony of defeat and joy of sweet victory circulate a most unique essence like none other I have ever been able to find. Deep within my heart lies a security in knowing that not only has my pride contributed to this essence, but that the blood, sweat and tears of players past have contributed to it as well. And we must not forget the ones who taught us what pride really means.

This is sacred to me; reminding me that I have given everything I ever had and put it all into the great game of basketball. I have given my heart and soul to this game. So whenever I leave my domain, I always take with me the anxiety and the yearning from deep within my soul that just can't wait until my next Return to Heaven."

❖

What Can You Do?

A lot of athletes, frustrated by losing or by not meeting their expectations in some other way, end up asking the same question: "But what can I do?" So, here is a brief answer that applies to just about all basketball players.

During games, you can sprint more, you can be more active off the ball on defense, you can be more alert, constantly asking yourself what is likely to happen next and constantly expecting a pass or a cut or a shot or a penetration. Also, you can encourage your teammates, bolster their confidence, and remind them of what needs to happen.

In practice, you can arrive earlier, work harder, care more about maximizing time, really try to use the time to improve—and then work to get your teammates to take the same approach as you.

Off the court, you can talk to your coach and talk to your teammates, keep your goals and your visions fresh in everyone's mind and keep reminding your teammates of what it takes to reach those goals. It is not enough to have goals; it is important that you have a plan for achieving those goals and that you keep everyone focused on doing the extra things that are necessary for success.

In the off-season, you have the best chance to have a huge impact on your future success. That's when you guarantee your improvement by shooting 500-1000 shots a day (all athletes can improve their shot), by lifting weights (no player is too strong), and by improving your skills with systematic practice and repetition. Once you commit to all that, then get your teammates to do it, too. It's a team game. You can't afford to mind your own business and hope for excellent, motivated teammates. You have to motivate your teammates and inspire excellence. Go by their houses, call them up, and pick them up. Talk to them, work with them, and share your dreams with them. There is so much you can do—and every day counts.

~ A message from Dick DeVenzio and the Point Guard Basketball College

❖

Little Hurts, Big Pictures

I get the chance to work with more than a thousand basketball players each year, and I keep in touch with enough of them to have become very familiar with a tremendous variety of problems that athletes deal with each season. They say their coaches don't understand them, or their teammates are lazy or not dedicated or jealous. . . the list goes on and on.

But the solution to most of the problems is the same most of the time. Athletes need to see the big picture, not dwell on the problems. At the time of a snub, or a lost opportunity, or a loss, or an injury, athletes have great difficulty seeing their lives in perspective. I try always to remind them: that's what is meant by adversity, not just opponents and tough games but all the things that go into sports. Nearly all teams and players have problems. But problems aren't the problem! Your response is what matters.

Keep in mind always that you are an athlete. Adversity is your sport, and it comes in many forms. Prepare for it, deal with it, and remember: your job is to learn to do your best, consistently, in spite of difficult circumstances. That is precisely what will earn you admiration and a sense of true worth. Though your problems seem big to you, deal with them calmly and intelligently. That's how you become a true champion.

~ Dick DeVenzio

Knowing Vs. Doing

EASY	VS	HARD
Knowing your role		Playing your role
Knowing what is right		Doing what is right
Jealousy		Praising a teammate
Wanting to win		Sacrificing to win
Making a commitment		Keeping a commitment

Taking on responsibility	Living up to responsibility
Criticizing	Trusting
I	Team
Wanting good grades	Studying
Taking	Giving
Pointing the finger	Blaming yourself
Hearing God's word	Living God's Word
Following the crowd	Standing Alone
Saying the right thing	Doing the right thing
Quitting	Perseverance

WHAT CAN YOU ADD TO THIS LIST?

~Coach Jerry Cypher

T *ogether*
E *veryone*
A *chieves*
M *ore*

Winner vs. Loser:

The Winner is always part of the answer;
The Loser is always part of the problem;

The Winner always has a program;

The Loser always has an excuse;

The Winner says, "Let me do it for you;"
The Loser says, "That's not my job;"

The Winner sees an answer for every problem;
The Loser sees a problem for every answer;

The Winner sees two open passes out of every trap;
The Loser sees two more defenders in the passing lanes;

The Winner says, "It may be difficult but it's possible;"
The Loser says, "It may be possible but it's too difficult."

Basketball

What I put into basketball is
what I get out of it.

~ Grant
Hill

Famous Quotes

Team spirit is what gives so many companies an edge over their competitors.

~ George L. Clements

❖

In life, as in football, you won't go far unless you know where the goalposts are.

~ Lou Holtz

❖

A man stopped to watch a Little League baseball game. He asked one of the youngsters what the score was. "We're behind eighteen to nothing," was the answer. "Well," said the man, "I must say you don't look discouraged."

"Discouraged?" the boy said, puzzled. "Why should we be discouraged? We haven't come to bat yet."

~ Author Unknown

❖

A word from the coach: I'm just a plow hand from Arkansas, but I have learned how to hold a team together, how to lift some men up, how to calm down others, until finally they've got one heartbeat together—a team.

There are just three things I'd ever say: If anything goes bad, I did it. If anything goes semi-good, then we did it. If anything goes real good, then you did it. That's all it takes to get people to win football games for you.

~ Bear Bryant

❖

The psychology instructor had just finished a lecture on mental health and was giving an oral test. Speaking specifically about manic depression, she asked, "How would you diagnose a patient who walks back and forth screaming at the top of his lungs one minute, then sits in a chair weeping uncontrollably the next?"

A young man in the rear raised his hand and answered, "A basket-ball coach?"

~ Author Unknown

❖

Individual honors are nice, but victory belongs to the team.

~ Red Auerbach

❖

The coach is the team, and the team is the coach; you reflect each other.

~ Sparky Anderson

❖

When a successful team becomes infected with the DISEASE OF ME, people who create 20% of the results begin believing they deserve 80% of the credit.

~ Author Unknown

❖

When I was young, I never wanted to leave the court until I got things exactly right!

~ Author Unknown

❖

To me, a great player is someone who gives it all they've got and makes the players around them better.

~ Karl Malone

❖

We play as a team. One-man teams are losing teams.

~ Kareem Abdul-Jabbar

❖

Winning is more related to good defense than good offense.

~ Jack Ramsey

❖

Winning never gets old.

~ John Havlicek

❖

Pressure is something you feel when you don't know what you're do-ing.

~ Peyton Manning

❖

Pressure is self-inflicted.

~ Tom Clements

❖

When you win, nothing hurts.

~ Joe Namath

❖

Coaching Tips

I would rather have a player who has mastered 2 or 3 moves than try to teach him 6 or 7.

~ Norm Sloan

❖

The most important job a coach does is to select personnel.

~ Norm Stewart

❖

I believe you win games by what you do from your first practice until your first game.

~ Jack Ramsey

❖

The more things we can get kids to do correctly off the court, the more they will do correctly on the court.

~ Mike Jarvis

❖

Practice structure determines success

~ Bob Knight

❖

Only praise behavior that you want to be repeated. Never use false praise.

~ Dean Smith

❖

If it doesn't bother you, it won't bother them.

~ Pat Summitt

We stop practice every time we see one of our players not blocking out.

~ Jim Calhoun

❖

You have to learn to learn to do the things you don't like. You have to like them. You have to learn to like the process. People who don't become successful say, "Well, I don't like doing that." Well, do you want to win? "Yeah, I want to win, but I don't like doing that." Well, you have to learn to like it.

~ Mike Krzyzewski

❖

We are more limited by our beliefs than our abilities. If you believe you are an average basketball player, you'll play like one. Believe you are a champion, and you'll eventually be one. Set your goal high and let them lift you up to where you really want to go.

~ Dr. Tom Amberry

❖

Nothing is work unless you'd rather be doing something else.

~ Dick Motta

❖

To players: play and practice like you are trying to make the team.

~ Mike Zrzyzewski

❖

Great effort springs naturally from great attitude.

~ Pat Riley

Those who work the hardest are the last to surrender.

~ Rick Pitino

Drugs

There is no place for the use of drugs by any athlete. Today we are in an environment where all types of drugs (stimulants and depressants to hard drugs) are readily accessible. And to say drugs are not present in athletics would be a falsehood, since it is a major concern at the professional as well as the collegiate and high school levels. However, you will find the people in athletics who use or have used drugs to enhance their performance have in the long run failed to excel and most have destroyed their careers. It can be noted that the people who are on top are there through hard work, intense desire and athletic ability.

We feel drugs should not be a part of your make up. Your association with those who do "use" drugs should be very minimal. You, your teammates and the basketball program will be judged and evaluated by those with who you associate. Self-discipline is definitely the key if you are going to be "straight" and great.

Many people will say marijuana is no worse than alcohol. We will not agree with that. But how bad is alcohol? Let's be frank. Alcohol is the villain in broken marriages, automobile accidents, disturbances, abandoned children, and many other problems. It causes physical damage to the liver, brain, and impairs the breathing function so that oxygen in the blood is decreased. We could go on and on with problems resulting from alcohol. We all admit it is an unsolved problem. Should we add another problem when we haven't been able to solve this one?

When people drink, usually they drink to be sociable, with no intention of getting drunk. But with marijuana, a person intends to get high, and more quickly than with alcohol. Marijuana causes distortion of depth and time perception. Marijuana slows everything down, while frequently causing a person to think things are sped up.

What Drinking and Drugs Will Do to Your Game

Drugs and alcohol are part of our culture. It's a shame, but it's true. It would be unrealistic to suggest otherwise. So the key for the serious athlete is to know just how devastating they can be to your career and your dreams.

Drugs and alcohol affect you in two ways—physically and mentally.

Physically, alcohol and other depressant drugs initially feel like stimulants because of their relaxing effects. But alcohol, in particular, displaces other energy sources in the diet while providing little or no nutritional benefit. High in calories, it causes marked imbalance of nutrients in the diet, as well as protein deficiency.

Alcohol causes changes in acid secretion, permeability of mucosa, and rate of gastric emptying in the stomach, which results in gastrointestinal damage. It impairs the uptake of fat, folate, vitamin B12 and thiamine and reduces your ability to digest lactose (milk) in the small intestine.

Athletes who use alcohol are more likely to develop pancreatitis, which results in poor fat and protein absorption, and an excess loss of fat and fat-soluble nutrients in the feces. Liver damage is also a danger for those who use alcohol. It causes diminished nutrient storage and an impaired ability to convert vitamins to metabolically useful forms.

Mentally, depressants can become psychologically addictive, causing you to lose the ability to concentrate as well as you should. And concentration is key to winning. More importantly, depressants and other drugs chip away at your character. Just as they blur reality, they blur your sense of self, causing you to lose respect and self-control. They ultimately leave you feeling worthless. And an athlete who believes he or she is worthless is an athlete who has no reason to win.

Finally, answer this question: how many people can you name, athletes or not, who have become great through the use of drugs and alcohol?

"Wise men learn by other men's mistakes, fools by their own."

~ H. G. Bohn

❖

The Len Bias Story

At 22, Len Bias had the world at his fingertips. He had worked hard all his life to achieve his dream of playing in the NBA. After a brilliant career at the University of Maryland, Bias' dream came true. In 1986, he was chosen in the first round by the Boston Celtics, the second pick in the draft overall. One week later, Len Bias was buried.

With a small group of friends in a campus dorm room, Len Bias was celebrating his hard-earned success. The mood was light, and he decided to try something he had never done before: cocaine.

Several hours later, Len Bias' heart stopped beating and his 6-foot, 8-inch frame collapsed. He never regained consciousness. It was later learned that cocaine had "shocked" his healthy heart into submission. It killed him.

Len Bias did cocaine once. But once was all it took. And that one foolish mistake cost him all the comfort and security his NBA contract would no doubt have provided. More importantly, that one foolish mistake cost him his dreams and his future. And to this day, people speak of Len Bias' life and death and shake their heads thinking about all the things he might have done.

What happened to Len Bias doesn't happen every day. But it does happen. And if you choose to use drugs or alcohol, you should know that there's a chance that you could be the next Len Bias.

Some Facts about Drugs

Drug use doesn't hurt only the user. Drug use endangers others by raising the risk of car crashes and other accidents. It also contributes to violent crime.

Addiction can happen quickly. It doesn't take months or years to become addicted to drugs or alcohol. And once you are addicted, it can be extremely difficult and painful to stop.

Drugs are dangerous for anyone. Even healthy, emotionally stable people can get into serious trouble through using drugs.

Drugs don't make you more confident. True self-confidence comes from within, not from a drug.

~ National Clearinghouse for Alcohol and Drug Information

Winner's Choice

REFERENCES FOR WINNING

MOVIES: **BOOKS:**

Rudy   *The Bible*

Rocky   *The Lou Holtz Story*
                                                     - Lou Holtz
Hoosiers   *The Winner Within*
                                                     - Pat Riley
Top Gun   *In the Trenches*
                                                     - Reggie White
The Natural   *Landing on My Feet*
                                                     - Kerry Strug
Apollo 13   *It Takes Commitment*
                                                     - Chad Hennings
Ghandi   *Eleven Seconds*
                                                     - Travis Roy
Mr. Holland's Opus   *A Season on the Mat*
                                                     - Nolan Zavoral
Glory   *Rebound*
                                                     - Bob Greene
Karate Kid   *Beyond Basketball*
                                                     - Coach Krzyzewski
8 Seconds   *The John Wooden Story*
                                                     - John Wooden
Chariots of Fire   *Future Shock*
                                                     - Alvin Toffler
Field of Dreams

V

The 'F' Word — FEAR

*The Dirtiest four letter word in the English
Language begins with the letter "F"
— Fear*

~ *Coach Jerry Cypher*

*We should not let our fears hold us back
from pursuing our hopes.*

~ *John F. Kennedy*

Success Will Never Come. . .
If You Are Afraid to Fail

The man who clings to certitudes, to the comfort of the familiar, to the seeming predictable, is not a man of faith. If everything is so sure and certain, there is no need of faith. Certitude permits passivity and immobility. Faith demands doing; faith demands acting, and action involves risk.

To laugh is to risk appearing the fool. To weep is to risk appearing sentimental. To reach out for another is to risk involvement. To expose feelings is to risk exposing your true self. To place your ideas and dreams before a crowd is to risk their rejection. To love is to risk not being loved in return. To live is to risk dying. To try at all is to risk failure.

But risk we must, for the greatest hazard to life is to risk nothing. The person who risks nothing does nothing, has nothing, and will accomplish nothing. He may avoid suffering and sorrow, but he simply cannot learn, change, grow, live, or love. Chained by his certitudes, existing as a slave, he has forfeited freedom. It is only the person who is willing to take risks who can truly be called a free man.

If

If you think that you're beaten, you are. If you think you dare not, you don't. If you like to win but think you can't, it's almost a clinch you won't.

If you think that you'll lose, you're lost. For out in the world we find success begins with a fellow's will; it's all in the state of mind.

If you think you're outclassed, you are. You've got to think high to rise. You've got to be sure of what you are before you can win the prize.

The battle of life not always goes to the strongest, fastest or smartest man. But sooner or later the man who wins, is the man who thinks he can.

If you can trust yourself though others doubt you and conquer fears that limit what you dare, so you can freely give to those about you the skills and talents that are yours to share.

If you can balance dreams with practicality and deal in facts, but never lose ideals, if you can face the harshness of reality and find the truths that prejudice conceals.

If you can be courageous when defeated and humble in the face of victory, or give your best till a task completed, however difficult that task may be.

If you can strive, not caring who gets credit, and work at building bridges and not walls, or hearing slander, just forget it and never fail to help someone that falls.

❖

Don't listen to those who say, "It's not done that way." Maybe it's not, but maybe you'll do it anyway. Don't listen to those who say, "You're taking too big a chance." Michelangelo would have painted the Sistine floor, and it would surely be rubbed out by today.

Most important, don't listen when the little voice of fear inside you rears its ugly head and says, "They're all smarter than you out there. They're more talented, they're taller, blonder, prettier and luckier and they have connections. They have a cousin who took out Meryl Streep's babysitter."

I firmly believe that if you follow a path that interests you, not to the exclusion of love, sensitivity, and cooperation with others, but with the strength of conviction that you can move others by your own efforts, and do not make success or failure the criteria by which you live, the chances are you'll be a person worthy of your own respect.

~ Playwright Neil Simon

Someone has said, "We only live 40 years of life. The rest is only commentary."

Someone else has said, "Today is my moment and now is my story."

The difference between the two is "change and challenge." "C" to it that your life is not merely a commentary of the past.

❖

Withdrawal from life is the result of our failure to cope with ideas—

ideas of ourselves, unreal ideas of others, or ideas that bear responsibilities. Hallucinations seem more inviting because they are not real.

We become a mixture of artificial ideas, moods, and feelings that tear us apart. Once we lose control of our realness, our life will be a continual "cop out." We'll find a pill or bottle for everything because fear has become our master.

Men and women with good health, jobs they like, and happy families are successes. That's what people who answered a Gallup poll believe are the real criteria of personal success. They ranked luxuries like expensive cars and houses at the bottom of the list.

The significance of money and possessions in today's society can't be overlooked. But, as this survey indicates, most people can distinguish the great difference between what they have and what they are.

Learn from the mistakes of others—you can never live long enough to make them all yourself.

Surveys indicate that certain traits are common to most successful people. These people:

- Have a purpose in life.
- Take risks and exercise control.
- Solve problems rather than place blame.
- Care about quality.
- Share their expertise and knowledge.

Rivers hardly ever run in a straight line. Rivers are willing to take ten thousand meanders and enjoy every one and grow from every one.

When rivers leave a meander they are always bigger than when they entered it.

When rivers meet an obstacle, they do not try to run over it—they merely go around, but they always get to the other side.

Rivers accept things as they are. They conform to the shape they find the world in, yet nothing changes things more than rivers.

Rivers move even mountains into the sea.

Rivers hardly ever are in a hurry, yet is there anything more likely to reach the point it sets out for than a river?

~ James Dillet Freeman

For every job that exists in the world there is someone somewhere who cannot do it. Given sufficient time and enough promotions, he will arrive eventually at that job and there he will remain—habitually bungling it, frustrating his co-workers, and eroding the efficiency of the organization.

~ The Peter Principle

Excellence is not the promotion to the top, but the achievement of our competence.

The first step toward excellence is to abhor mediocrity. If we sit smug and satisfied in the darkness of apathy, our potential will never see daylight.

Perseverance is the backbone of excellence. It is easy to "cop out" and "give up" with an apathetic cry of self-pity. The pursuit of excellence is difficult, and it takes a courageous person to make the journey.

Courage takes the risk of failure, of making a wrong decision, and of suffering the consequences that follow.

But courage relies on God. It says: "With God on my side, I can do anything,"

❖

Everyone has inside himself. . .
A piece of good news!
The good news is that you really don't know:

- How great you can be
- How much you can love
- What you can accomplish
- What your potential is.

How can you top good news like that?

~ Anne Frank

❖

People on an average use only 10 percent of their creative potential. They do not develop more than the minimum and yet they have re-sources to attain the maximum. They groan for fulfillment but fail to meet the challenge of their own power because they lack the basic desire to be better than they are.

You may be disappointed if you fail, but you are doomed if you don't try.

~ Beverly Sills

❖

Once you start believing, there's nothing you can't do!

❖

One, who lacks the courage to start, is already finished.

❖

People don't fail, they give up!

❖

Only those who dare to fail greatly can ever achieve greatly.
~ Robert F. Kennedy

❖

Courage is doing what you're afraid to do. There can be no courage unless you're scared.
~ Eddie Rickenbacker

❖

Occasional failure is the price of improvement.

❖

You cannot succeed without believing in yourself, and that belief is completely under your control.
~ Karch Kiraly

❖

No one can make you feel inferior, unless you agree with it.
~ Eleanor Roosevelt

❖

There is no failure except in no longer trying.

❖

Getting started is often the hardest part of a job. We need all our energy just for the starting. We're like cars—only a small percentage of an engine's power is necessary to run a car, but all its power may be necessary to start it.

I don't like to lose, and that isn't so much because it is just a football game, but because the defeat means the failure to reach your objective. The trouble in American life today, in business as well as in sports, is that too many people are afraid of competition. The result is that in some circles people have come to sneer at success if it costs hard work and training and sacrifice.

~ Knute Rockne

An old sheepherder stood looking at a flock of sheep in a field. "Look," said his companion, "those sheep have been sheared."

The old man continued peering at the sheep for a moment, and then said, "sheared on this side anyway."

A certain amount of caution is a virtue, yet, as a wise man once observed, "Few great undertakings in this world would ever get off the ground without faith in things not known."

Lord Nelson, England's famous naval hero, suffered from sea sickness throughout his entire life. Needless to say, the man who destroyed Napoleon's fleet did not let it interfere with his career. He not only learned to live with this personal weakness, he conquered it.

Most of us have our own little "sea sicknesses" too. For some it may be physical, for others psychological. Usually, it's a private war, carried on quietly within us. No one will pin a medal on us for winning it, but nothing can dim the satisfaction of knowing we did not surrender.

Grove Patterson, editor of the *Toledo Blade* many years ago, always thought that the slang expression, "So what?" had real value.

"I have an idea," Patterson once wrote, "that we can apply it to about fifty percent of our troubles, and find that it is a comfortable cure-all.

"I know a so-called big industrialist who is forever worrying about trivialities," said Patterson. "He is constantly engaged in postmortems. The right answer, which he doesn't know, to practically all his fulminations is "so what?"

"I am the frequent victim of my own postmortems," said Patterson. "I sometimes lie awake nights trying to figure out why I did this or that, or didn't do it, and all the time the easy conclusion is within my grasp, "so what?"

"Many of us complain because of our lot in life when it is evident that there is little we can do about it. "So what?" We didn't ask to be born, but here we are, "so what?" Others complain about circumstances which they could change if they had the courage and the energy. These people really don't have much use for this phrase. I speak mostly of and for those who seek to re-pour the water that has gone under the bridge. When we finally come to learn that many things come to all of us that we cannot do anything about, we shall have put a broad and sturdy plank into the foundation of our philosophy."

VI

Never Give Up

A diamond is nothing more
than a lump of coal that stuck to its task!

~ B. C. Forbes

NEVER GIVE UP

Never,

Never,

Never,

Never,

Never,

Never,

Never,

Never,

Never,

Never,

Never give up!

~ Winston Churchill

You Mustn't Quit

When things go wrong, as they sometimes will,
When the road you're trudging seems all uphill,
When the funds are low and the debts are high,
And you want to smile, but you have to sigh,
When care is pressing you down a bit,
Rest if you must—but never quit.

Life is queer, with its twists and turns,
As every one of us sometimes learns,
And many a failure turns about,
When he might have won if he'd stuck it out,
Stick to your task, though the pace seems slow,
You may succeed with one more blow.

Success is failure turned inside out,
The silver tint of the clouds of doubt,
And you never can tell how close you are,
It may be near, when it seems afar,
So stick to the fight when you're hardest hit,
It's when things seem worst that YOU MUSN'T QUIT.

Perseverance:

    Perseverance is the action or condition of persisting in a state, enterprise, or undertaking in spite of counter influences, opposition or discouragement.

By perseverance the snail reached the ark.
~ Charles Haddon

IN THE BLEACHERS   By Steve Moore

TOUGH TIMES DON'T LAST:
TOUGH PEOPLE DO!

~ Steve Moore

Don't Quit

Don't quit when
The tide is the lowest,
For it's just about to turn;
Don't quit over doubts
And questions,
For there's something
You may learn.

Don't quit when
The night is darkest,
For it's just awhile 'til dawn;
Don't quit when you've
Run the farthest,
For the race is almost won.

Don't quit when
The hill is steepest,
For your goal
Is almost nigh;
Don't quit, for you're
Not a failure
Until you fail to try.

When You're Lost

When you're lost in the wild,
And you're scared as a child,
And death looks you long in the eye,
And you're as sore as a boil,
It's according to Hoyle,
"To cock your revolver and...die."

Not the code of man says,
"Fight all you can"
And self-destruction
is barred.
In hunger and woe, Oh,
It's easy to blow.
It's the hell reserved,
For the Break Fast that's hard.

(You're sick of the game!)
Well now that's a shame.
You're young and you're brave,

And you're bright.
You had a raw deal
I know, but squeal.
Buck up.
Do your damnedest And fight.

It's the plugging away,
That will win you the day.
So don't be a piker, old pard!
Just draw on your grit,
It's so easy to quit.
It's the keeping your chin up that's hard.

It's easy to cry,
That you're beaten and die,
It's easy to crawfish and craw.
But to fight and fight,
When hope is out of sight,
Well that's the best game of all,

And though you come out,
Of each grueling bout,
All beaten, and broken and tired,
Just have one more try,
It's dead easy to die,
It's the keeping on living that's hard.

It is not the critic who counts, not the man who points out how the strong man stumbled or where the doer of deeds could have done better. The credit belongs to the man who is actually in the arena; whose face is marred by dust and sweat and blood; who strives valiantly; who errs and comes short again and again; who knows the great enthusiasms, the great devotions, and spends himself in a worthy cause; who, at the best, knows in the end the triumph of high achievement; and who, at the worst, if he fails, at least fails while daring greatly, so that his place shall never be with those cold and timid souls who know neither victory nor defeat.

~ Theodore Roosevelt

Nothing in this world can take the place of persistence. Talent will not; nothing is more common than unsuccessful people with talent. Genius will not; unrewarded genius is almost a proverb. Education will not; the world is full of educated derelicts. Persistence and determination alone are omnipotent. The slogan "press on" has solved and always will solve the problems of the human race.

~ Calvin Coolidge

The marvelous richness of human experience would lose something of rewarding joy if there were no limitations to overcome. The hilltop hour would not be so wonderful if there were no dark valleys to traverse.

~ Helen Keller

Life is like an onion: you peel it off one layer at a time and sometimes you weep.

If we intend to experience life to its fullest, then we can expect suffering. Our love might be rejected, promises broken, dreams shattered, and health impaired.

But when we write our memoirs, the sweet taste of a full life with its few bitter tears will spell out our experience of satisfaction.

Suffering is not our worst experience. A meaningless life without a sense of satisfaction is the most unbearable.

~ Carl Sandburg

In a small pub in the highlands of Scotland a group of fishermen gathered one afternoon and were enjoying a round of ale. Just as one was showing with his hands how big one fish was that had gotten away, a waitress passed. His hand hit a glass of ale she was carrying on a tray and some of the dark brew spilled on the white wall of the pub. It began to run down. The waitress hastily took a cloth from her apron and began to wipe, but the ale had already left an ugly dark stain.

At another table, a man rose and came over. He took a crayon from his pocket and as all in the pub watched, began to sketch around the stain. In a few moments, he had drawn the head of a magnificent stag with spreading antlers. Under his hand, the mistake had become a thing of beauty. The artist was Sir Edwin Landseer. At that time he was England's foremost painter of animals.

Mistakes occur in our lives and yet, it seems that there are always those who can take a mistake, turn it around, and make something good come from it.

Although Henry Matisse was nearly thirty years younger than Auguste Renoir, the two great artists were dear friends and frequent companions. When Renoir was confined to his home during the last decade of his life, Matisse visited him daily.

Renoir, almost paralyzed by arthritis, continued to paint in spite of his infirmities. One day, as Matisse watched the elder painter working in his studio fighting tortuous pain with each brush stroke, he blurted out: "Auguste, why do you continue to paint when you are in such agony?"

Renoir answered simply: "The beauty remains; the pain passes." And so, almost to his dying day, Renoir put paint to canvas. One of his most famous paintings, *The Bathers*, was completed just two years before his passing, fourteen years after he was stricken by this disabling disease.

One of the biggest money-makers in the movie industry has been Arnold Schwarzenegger. But if he had taken some advice given him years ago, you might never have heard of him.

Schwarzenegger had won the Mr. Universe title numerous times competing with other weight lifters and bodybuilders, but he wanted to break into acting.

"I went to look for an agent and it was almost impossible," said Schwarzenneger. "I remember a guy told me, 'Listen, stay with bodybuilding. You have an accent, a body that's too overdeveloped for films, and a strange name that nobody can pronounce.'"

I said to myself, "Well, isn't that typical? I met the same resistance in bodybuilding, where everyone said, 'Why do you want to do that? It's an American sport. A little Austrian farm boy, and you think you're going to win the American Mr. Universe title? Forget it.'"

"Fortunately, by then I knew it didn't matter what people said. So I pursued acting. I knew it could happen if I worked on my talent and my accent. I thought eventually some people would learn to spell my name and even pronounce it. And, I told myself, if they do, they'll never forget it, because it's hard to forget once you learn a hard name."

❖

Everything that is done in the world is done by hope.
~ Martin Luther

❖

Failures come to all of us. No matter how hard we try, sometimes things will go wrong. Success is oftenest gained through long striving, though occasionally it is reached with less difficulty. After all, the harder we have to work for the attainment of an object, the more we appreciate it when it is in our possession. Do not be discouraged because of failures; begin over. Throughout the entire world people are beginning over; there is not a household but has learned the lesson. There is rebuilding done at all times of the year—a pulling down of half-finished plans, a ripping out of false stitches and a new start being made. Take fresh courage, and try again, no matter how hard it may be.

Break a spider's web, and she will set to work immediately to repair the damage; rob a beehive, and the little occupants will go on making cells and gathering fresh stores of honey; brush down an anthill, and the busy little ants will go to cleaning out the rubbish and rebuilding the demolished house at once. It is always creditable to be willing to begin over.
~ Ida Scott Taylor

❖

Springdale Graduate Overcomes Cancer to Play College Football

by Paul Kogut

Like A Rock:

Now that the battle to save his life is over, Brian Godfrey is looking forward to resuming the battle for a starting job on the Slippery Rock football team.

After 12 chemotherapy treatments and many nights worrying if he ever would play football again, Godfrey, a 1999 Springdale High School graduate, is practicing at nose guard for The Rock.

He probably won't start because senior nose guard Ian Anderson, a Freeport graduate, is a two-time all-conference pick. However, it's a victory in itself that he's able to participate in an athletic activity as physically demanding as a Division II football preseason camp.

Godfrey's return to regular-season football will come in memorable surroundings.

Slippery Rock opens the season against Florida Atlantic at 4 p.m. on Saturday at Pro Player Stadium home of the Miami Dolphins.

"This is something you look forward to when you're playing in high school or junior high," said Godfrey, now 20 years old and listed at 6'-2" and 275 pounds in the Slippery Rock media guide.

"To get on a plane, and then play at a pro stadium, it's a dream. I've been looking forward to it ever since the coaches came to my house right after they heard about (the schedule). They told me right after I got diagnosed."

Godfrey's radiologist has declared him "clinically and radiographically without evidence of disease" in a written report to the family. Doctors have cleared him to play college football.

For the next year, Godfrey will be tested every four months. As long as he stays healthy, the frequency of his required exams will decrease over the following four years.

"I hear so many terms myself, I'm not exactly sure," Godfrey said about the status of his cancer. "All I care about is they tell me I'm all right and I can play. It's in remission? It's dead? All I know is they gave me a clean bill of health. And that's all that's important to me."

His mother, Bonnie, and father, Philip, plan to attend the Slippery Rock opener in Miami.

"Brian isn't one to talk about things," Bonnie said. "He didn't want to be known as the kid with cancer. He wanted to be known as the kid who beat it."

Then she laughed. "What he really wants to be known as is a defensive lineman. He's getting his chance."

Blind-sided:

Godfrey can think back on a time when he shrugged off his fatigue. He wouldn't let the challenges of making the transition from high school football to the college game get to him.

He wouldn't show weakness. Not when he was coming off a red-shirt freshman season at Slippery Rock and battling for a starting role on the defensive line.

Still, it had been an exhausting 2000 spring camp for Godfrey.

At certain practices, the coaches let him know they were unhappy with his play. Godfrey was happy to be headed for his Cheswick home. But pain in Godfrey's left armpit wouldn't cease and the lump wouldn't go away. The hulking lineman thought he might have damaged a muscle while lifting weights in excess of 350 pounds.

He decided to have the lump examined by a doctor. The doctor recognized something more serious than a weight-lifting injury. Godfrey was sent for a biopsy and that revealed a form of cancer called Hodgkin's disease.

Immediately, a series of chemotherapy was scheduled. Godfrey's life as a healthy 19-year-old athlete was knocked as flat as a pancaked lineman.

His battle to start at Slippery Rock would have to wait. The effort to save his life would begin.

Season of Pain:

Godfrey expected to spend the 2000 college football season in helmet and pads. Instead, he had a "port" through which anti-cancer drugs could be fed into his body, implanted in his right pectoral muscle.

Godfrey asked the doctors to position the bottle cap-sized device so as not to impede weightlifting. Depending on how he felt, he would pump iron for about an hour twice a week.

"He never stopped lifting weights, even during chemotherapy." Bonnie said. "That was his goal. That's how focused he was."

Godfrey bench pressed more than 350 pounds during his illness.

"I wanted to keep in the best shape I could," he said. "The plan all along was to come back and play football again."

Godfrey went through the chemotherapies once every couple of weeks. The first was in June and the last in November. Each session lasted about an hour and half.

"They hook you up, and you have to wait until the drugs drip into you," he said, referring to the tube attached to the port in his chest.

"It wears on you, physically and mentally." The drugs attacked his cancer but didn't eliminate his fatigue or nausea. He was told he might lose his hair. He felt lucky when he didn't. "Everybody's always complaining about football camp," Bonnie said. "He's been through chemo-therapy."

Getting a Lift:

The disappointment of sitting out a season also was weighing on Godfrey's mind as last fall approached. That is until an old friend came calling.

Springdale coach Chuck Wagner, who started Godfrey on the offensive and defensive lines, had lunch with his ex-player and then asked him if he would like to be an assistant coach, even though he didn't have a paid position available. Godfrey accepted.

"I was happy as heck to have him as a volunteer." Wagner said. "The idea crossed my mind when I found out he wasn't going to be staying at school. I guess they thought it was best for him to leave school and the team because his resistance was down."

"I thought Brian could help us, and the program could help him by keeping his mind off a tough situation." Godfrey primarily worked with the Springdale linemen. The Dynamo seniors were only sophomores in Godfrey's last season of high school football.

"He did a super job," Wagner said "The young kids loved him and looked up to him." Still, Godfrey was zapped by nausea and fatigue.

At times, he decided not to ride the team bus and traveled by car instead because he would become ill and didn't want to slow the team or let the players see him in that condition.

"Honestly, never once did he complain or look for any sympathy," Wagner said. "He was extremely upbeat and positive. I just couldn't be happier or more proud of the way he hung in there."

Godfrey didn't just show up when football drills opened this summer. "Brian came in prepared, physically," Slippery Rock defensive coordinator Jay Foster said. "He's in phenomenal shape. He's an athlete right now, and he's a big one."

Godfrey benched a personal-high 445 pounds during camp. Foster said he thinks being an assistant coach helped Godfrey develop into a better player. The young player sees things from both viewpoints now. And Godfrey's attitude is topnotch according to Foster.

"Brian doesn't feel sorry for himself," he said. "Camp doesn't scare him because of what he's been through." Godfrey agrees. "I don't take it for granted anymore." He said, "I'm happy to be playing again."

Community Unity:

Godfrey and Godfrey alone battled his cancer. But he said he won't forget the warm smiles and well wishes he received during his struggle.

They bolstered his spirit.

"Everyone was so supportive and great," he said. "My friends, family and coaches, I got letters from people on the (Slippery Rock) team. The coaches came to my house and visited me. My friends would come over and cheer me up. That helped a lot."

The Slippery Rock team honored Godfrey by wearing his jersey number (98) on their helmets during the 2000 season. "I think a football team is an interesting group," Foster said. "It's one of the few sports in which you literally bleed with each other."

The guys have accepted him back. I don't think they talk about it a whole bunch. But just about every week, when Brian was sick, if somebody didn't visit, somebody called. It would be the same if a family member was sick.

Members of Godfrey's church, Cheswick Presbyterian, marked his recovery. After completing his final chemotherapy, he was called to the front during Sunday service and congratulated with a football shaped balloon and plaque.

Foster said he felt guilty after Godfrey was diagnosed with cancer because he "rode him pretty hard." in practice during the 2000 spring sessions.

He adds that Godfrey doesn't want his teammates to take it easy on him. "People are taking shots at him when they can." Foster said. "They're all competing. He's a very proud kid. When you see a guy like that, you shut up and don't worry about your little aches and pains."

Godfrey is indulging in his passion – football. But his victory over cancer is far greater than any he could earn on the football field.

"What he's done is so inspirational," Wagner said. "Everybody connected with the school and the community has nothing but a high regard for Brian.

❖

Nobody ever gave Bret Butler a chance of playing major league baseball. That's exactly the way Bret liked it.

He was a standout in high school, but the scholarships didn't come. So he walked on with over 200 other hopefuls at Arizona State, one of the best collegiate baseball programs in the NCAA. Eight made it, and Bret was one of them. He later transferred to a little college in Oklahoma that offered him a scholarship and became a two-time All-American.

He was passed over in the major league draft, until the 23rd round and then selected only as a favor to his high school coach. His pay was $1,000 a month.

But Bret had a little secret. It was the same one he had used throughout his life. He knew he was good. He was driven. And the doubts were his fuel. And all along, through the slights, he could hear his father's voice, telling him to believe in himself and avoid the regret of not giving it everything that he could.

And Bret went into a stellar career with the Los Angeles Dodgers. He played for 17 years. He wears a World Series ring. He hit .300 five times. He had 5,400 hits.

For Bret it was always about discipline—being the first on the field, the last to leave. He was too small, so he learned how to lay down bunts. That was his game: compensating, adjusting, finding a way.

Bret had it all—fame, a multi-million dollar contract and a beautiful family. He also would find out he had cancer. The invincible athlete, the little guy who beat the odds, was told that his career was over.

He was angry at first. He questioned God and shut himself off from his family. Ironically, it was in his faith and in his family that he found his strength. And he found his perspective in the lifelong advice his father had given him. The advice that had carried him over, around and through every other obstacle he had met in his life. So he asked the doctor what his odds were of beating the cancer. The doctor told him the truth: one in 5,000. For a guy like Bret, that was good news. He knew his odds of playing professional baseball were over one in 10,000. The battle was on.

Bret began an extensive treatment and rehab program, pushing himself to rid his body of the cancer and get himself back into major league form. He leaned on his faith and his family. He recalled the mental discipline of his time as an All-State wrestler. He remembered every doubt that had ever been cast his way.

The challenge also crystallized his understanding of himself as an athlete. Bret had seen all the mistakes: the obsessions, the egos and the divorces. He saw athletes who had no respect for the heritage and gifts of the game and who only understood the obsession of putting it before everything else. Bret remembered what he loved about baseball, what it had done for him and where its priority lies.

And like he always had, Bret beat the odds.

On his first at bat after the rehab, a pitch slammed into Bret's hand, smashing a number of bones.

Bret had nothing left to prove. He was a mature man who was closing the door on an outstanding athletic career. And he understood that there were other things in his life that deserve just as much commitment as he had made to his baseball career. There were no regrets because Bret had followed good advice, giving it everything he had. After 17 years of accomplishment, it was time to move on, because as Bret Butler will tell you, "God was telling him to rest for a while."

The only place you can win a game is on the field. The only place you can lose it is in your mind and heart.

~ Darrell Royal

It's a rare person who doesn't get discouraged. Whether it happens to us or to an associate we're trying to cheer up, the answer centers around one word: perseverance.

The value of courage, persistence, and perseverance has rarely been illustrated more convincingly than in the life story of this man (his age appears in the column on the right:

Failed in business at the age of	22
Ran for Legislature—defeated	23
Again failed in business	24
Elected to Legislature	25
Sweetheart died	26
Had a nervous breakdown	27
Defeated for Speaker	29
Defeated for Elector	31
Defeated for Congress	34
Elected to Congress	37
Defeated for Congress	39
Defeated for Senate	46
Defeated for Vice President	47
Defeated for Senate	49
Elected President of the United States	51

That's the record of Abraham Lincoln.

Thomas Edison, probably America's greatest inventor, was born on February 11, 1847, in Milan, Ohio. When he first attended school in Port Huron, Michigan, his teachers complained that he was "too slow" and hard to handle. As a result, Edison's mother decided to take her son out of school and teach him at home. Young Edison disliked arithmetic intensely, but he was fascinated by science. At ten he had already set up his first chemistry laboratory.

Edison's inexhaustible energy and genius (which he allegedly defined as "one percent inspiration and ninety-nine percent perspiration") eventually produced in his lifetime more than 1,300 inventions.

If you have experienced a setback, don't despair. Assess yourself. Make a list of your strengths. Then seek out companies that might be able to use your skills.

Even if you have a job, but feel stymied, you can go through the same process. Aim at jobs that require your skills. Concentrate on what you can do well. Jo Farrell did it. You may be able to do it, too.

"I wish I were honest enough to admit all my shortcomings:
Brilliant enough to accept flattery without it making me arrogant;
Tall enough to tower above deceit;
Strong enough to treasure love;
Brave enough to welcome criticism;
Compassionate enough to understand human frailties;
Wise enough to recognize my mistakes;
Humble enough to appreciate greatness;
Staunch enough to stand by my friends;
Human enough to be thoughtful of my critics."

~ Joe Farrell

Tomorrow:

There's a whole day tomorrow that hasn't been tried.
A day when new courage flings old fears aside.
A new dawn that's coming to bring a nobler noon.
Today may be troubled; tomorrow's here soon.

There's a whole day tomorrow that hasn't been tried
With hours un-wasted and hopes still un-denied.
Free from fret or folly, it lies untouched, yet near.
Today's page is blotted, tomorrow's is clear.

❖

There's always a way to rise, there's always a way to advance, but the road that leads to Mount Success does not come by way of chance. It goes through the valley of work and strives, through the stations of persever-ance. And the one who succeeds while others fail must be willing to pay most dear.

There's always a way to fall, there's always a way to slide, and those you find at the foot of the hill all sought for an easy ride. And so on and up, though the road may be thick and fast, there's room at the top for the one who tries and victory comes at last!

❖

One of the pitfalls people over forty falls into is thinking that it's too late. It's an old cliché, but the simple fact is that it's rarely too late for anything.

Some years ago a man over sixty was offered nearly $200,000 for a restaurant-motel-service station business that he'd spent his life building up. He turned the offer down because he loved the business and wasn't ready to retire yet.

Two years later, at age sixty-five, he was flat broke with no income to look forward to but a small Social Security check each month. The state had built a new highway bypassing his business and he lost it. Most people would have been crushed by such a blow, but he refused to give up.

Instead, he took stock. There was one thing he knew how to do—fry chicken. Maybe he could sell that knowledge to others. He kissed his wife good-bye and in a battered old car, with a pressure cooker, a can of spe-cially prepared flour, set out to sell his idea to others restaurants. It was tough going and he often slept in the car because there wasn't enough money for a hotel room.

A few years later he had built a nationwide franchised restaurant chain called Kentucky Fried Chicken. The man was Colonel Sanders.

❖

People who stand still may avoid stubbing their toes, but they won't make much progress. Every company, every department needs super-vi-sors with the courage to try new ideas and run the risk of making mistakes. Otherwise, progress never happens.

"The better a man is, the more mistakes he will make, for the more new things he will try," says management consultant, Peter Drucker. "I would never promote into a top-level job a man who was not making mistakes. . . otherwise he is sure to be mediocre."

❖

Develop a train of thought on which to ride. The nobility of your life, as well as your happiness, depends upon the direction in which that train of thought is going.

When we have developed a philosophy of life, it is easy to make decisions. Energy then enforces each decision.

If we know what we want to accomplish and desire it enough, then neither fear, doubt nor ridicule can stop us.

~ Dr. Lawrence Peter

❖

Physical ailments, rejection, depression and anxiety—these are in-ev-itable realities of the human condition. We can let them tear us apart or we can accept them for what they are. They can transform, mature, and educate us.

Acceptance should absorb pain like a sponge. It comes from the overwhelming desire to enjoy life in spite of suffering. It neither lashes out in blame nor turns inwardly toward self-pity. It realizes that suffering is an experience of the human condition, and if we are to "feel human" we must "feel suffering."

Solitude

Laugh, and the world laughs with you;
Weep, and you weep alone.
For the sad old earth must borrow its mirth,
But has trouble enough of its own.
Sing, and the hills will answer;
Sigh, it is lost on the air.
The echoes bound to a joyful sound,
But shrink from voicing care.

Rejoice, and men will seek you;
Grieve, and they turn and go,
They want full measure of all your pleasure,
But they do not need your woe.
Be glad, and your friends are many;
Be sad, and you lose them all.
There are none to decline your nectar wine,
But alone you must drink life's gall.

Feast, and your halls are crowded;
Fast, and the world goes by.
Succeed and give, and it helps you live,
But no man can help you die.
There is room in the halls of pleasure,
For a long and lordly train,
But one by one we must move on,
Through the narrow aisles of pain.

VII

SHORT STORIES AND LIFE LESSONS

Every day, ordinary people do extraordinary things.

If you can dream it, you can do it.

Today is your turn.

Michael Sovern, the president of Columbia University, has announced that he will resign, effective next June. A reporter asked Sovern if there were any task he had left incomplete.

"Yes," replied Sovern. "It sounds complacent, but there is really only one." He was referring to the lack of instruction in ethics and values for the average student. Professional schools, he pointed out, like law, medical and business administration, have some pretty good programs in values and professional ethics. The average undergraduate, however, gets no training in these areas.

Why? Most likely because most educators—from grammar school through college—are afraid to touch the subjects. Topics such as these are usually addressed by parents or members of religious organizations. That's why the average educator wants no part of them. Let others stick their necks out! The result is that in this country, young people who need moral and ethical training more than ever, are getting less than ever.

Morals and ethics are not a religion. They are logical, sensible principles of good conduct regardless of anyone's religion. We need these for a peaceful, productive society. Until we realize this, and start teaching these principles again in our families and our schools, our society will continue on a one-way street—downhill.

When Thomas Jefferson created the state-run University of Virginia, he insisted it have no religious affiliation. Yet even with this restriction, he still included "moral philosophy" in the required course of study.

We live in a country that has made a fetish of freedom of religion. It now bars religious material of any kind in its public schools. But couldn't we teach good morals and ethics not as religion, but simply as the most practical, direct route to success and happiness? And hadn't we better do it soon?

~ John L. Beckley

Elbert Hubbard once said, "A retentive memory may be a good thing, but the ability to forget is the true token of greatness."

Successful people forget. They know the past is irrevocable. They're running a race. They can't afford to look behind. Their eye is on the finish line.

Magnanimous people forget. They're too big to let little things disturb them. They forget easily. If anyone does them wrong, they consider the source and keep cool. It's only the small people who cherish revenge.

Be a good forgetter. Business dictates it, and success demands it.

When we think of creativity, we tend to picture a composer or an artist at work on a masterpiece. But creativity is simply a new approach to anything.

Earle Dickson, an employee of Johnson & Johnson, married a young woman who was accident-prone.

Johnson & Johnson sold large surgical dressings in individual packages, but these were not practical for small cuts and burns. Dickson put a small wad of sterile cotton and gauze in the center of an adhesive strip to hold it in place.

Finally, tired of making up these little bandages every time one was needed, he got the idea of making them in quantity and using crinoline fabric to temporarily cover the adhesive strip. When the bandage was needed, the two pieces of crinoline could easily be peeled off, producing a small, ready-to-use bandage.

The firm's president, James Johnson, saw Dickson put one of his homemade bandages on his finger. Impressed by its convenience, he decided to start mass-producing them under the name Band-Aids.

Dickson had been looking for a way to handle a small problem, and in the process he invented a useful new product.

❖

Robert Louis Stevenson suffered in poor health from childhood right up until he died at age 44. But he never allowed illness to conquer his spirit. He felt that being happy was a duty and he faithfully followed a number of precepts to keep him as happy as possible. Here they are:

- Make up your mind to be happy. Learn to find pleasure in simple things.

- Make the best of your circumstances. No one has everything, and everyone has some sorrow mixed in with the gladness of life. The trick is to make the laughter outweigh the tears.

- Don't take yourself too seriously. Don't think that somehow you should be protected from misfortunes that befall other people.

- Don't let criticism worry you. You can't please everybody.

- Don't let others set your standards. Be yourself.

- Do the things you enjoy doing, but don't go into debt in the process.

- Don't borrow trouble. Imaginary things are harder to bear than the actual ones.

- Do not cherish enmities. Don't hold grudges. Hatred poisons the soul.

- Have many interests. If you can't travel, read about many places.

- Don't spend your life brooding over sorrows or mistakes. Don't be one who never gets over things.

- Do what you can for those less fortunate than yourself.

- Keep busy at something. A very busy person never has time to be unhappy.

Stanley Arnold was a man with million dollar ideas. Some years ago, Arnold was managing one of his father's fifteen Pick-N-Pay stores in Cleveland, Ohio, when a blizzard hit town. The city was paralyzed, and all fifteen stores were empty. Employees who had reported to work didn't have much to do, until Arnold came up with his idea. He had the employees make snowballs—7,900 of them. Then he had the snowballs packed into grapefruit crates and transported to a deep-freeze facility. Then he asked the Weather Bureau when he could expect the hottest day of the year.

They told him mid-July. Armed with this information, Arnold took a train to New York and went to see Charles Mortimer, then president of General Foods. He proposed a joint promotional sale of General Food's newly introduced Birds Eye frozen foods. The sale was to be held in mid-July, and young Mr. Arnold wanted General Foods to provide an array of prizes. The sale was to be called, "A Blizzard of Values." As his contribution, Arnold proposed to give away snowballs.

General Foods agreed to cooperate. Summer came, and it turned out to be 100 degrees on the sale date. Police had to be called to control the crowds. During the five days of Pick-N-Pay's "Blizzard of Values," some 40,000 General Foods samples were given away, along with 7,900 grapefruit-sized snowballs. Thousands of customers were introduced to the new products, and the food industry discovered what excitement could do for sales.

~ Stanley Arnold

Mary Kay Ask, founder and director of the highly successful Mary Kay Cosmetics firm, says women are the greatest unused resource this country has. Women are the major factor in the firm's success, and its founder has mastered the art of bringing out the best in them.

It begins, says Ms. Ash, with the Golden rule—doing unto others as you'd have them do unto you. "You'll always be fair to people," she explains, "if you put yourself in their shoes and consider what their reaction will be to things."

Another facet of her formula for success involves encouraging people. "Forget their mistakes," she advised, "and zero in on one small thing they do right. Praise them and they'll do more things right and discover talents and abilities they never realized they had."

~ Mary Kay Ash

In the days when an ice cream sundae cost much less, a 10-year-old boy entered a hotel coffee shop and sat at a table. A waitress put a glass of water in front of him. "How much is an ice cream sundae?"

"Fifty cents," replied the waitress.

The little boy pulled his hand out of his pocket and studied a number of coins in it. "How much is a dish of plain ice cream?" he inquired.

Some people were now waiting for a table and the waitress was a bit impatient. "Thirty five cents," she said brusquely. The little boy again counted the coins. "I'll have the plain ice cream." he said.

The waitress brought the ice cream, put the bill on the table, and walked away. The boy finished the ice cream, paid the cashier, and departed. When the waitress came back, she picked up the empty plate and then swallowed hard at what she saw. There placed neatly beside the empty dish, were two nickels and five pennies – her tip.

General Eisenhower used to demonstrate the art of leadership with a simple piece of string. He'd put it on a table and say: *Pull* it and it'll follow wherever you wish. *Push* it and it will go nowhere at all. It's just that way when it comes to leading people.

Leadership isn't something that comes automatically just because you have people working for you. Leadership depends on followers. If people don't follow a manager's lead voluntarily – if they always have to be forced – that person is not a good leader.

What do you think the "job" of leadership really is? Is it to tell those who work for you exactly what you want done. . . and to stay on top of them until they do it? If that's how you see your job, you don't have the viewpoint it takes to lead successfully. Leadership depends on the ability to make people *want* to follow—voluntarily.

~ General Eisenhower

You can buy people's time; you can buy their physical presence at a given place; you can even buy a measured number of their skilled muscular motions per hour. But you cannot buy enthusiasm. . . you cannot buy loyalty. . . you cannot buy the devotions of hearts, minds, or souls. You must earn these.

~ Clarence Francis

Dr. Karl Menninger, the famous psychiatrist, once gave a lecture on mental health and was answering questions from the audience.

"What would you advise a person to do," asked one man, "if that person felt a nervous breakdown coming on?"

Most people expected him to reply: "Consult a psychiatrist." To their astonishment, he replied: "Lock up your house, go across the railway tracks, find someone in need and do something to help that person."

~ Dr. Karl Menninger

❖

In 1886, Karl Benz drove through the streets of Munich, Germany. The car was the forerunner of today's Mercedes Benz.

The machine angered the citizens, because it was noisy and scared the children and horses. Pressured by the citizens, the local officials immediately established a speed limit for "horseless carriages" of 3½ miles an hour in the city limits, and 7 miles an hour outside.

Benz knew he could never develop a market for his car and compete against horses if he had to creep along at those speeds, so he invited the mayor of the town for a ride. The mayor accepted. Benz than arranged for a milkman to park his horse and wagon on a certain street and, as Benz and the mayor drove by, to whip up his old horse and pass them, and as he did so to give the German equivalent of the Bronx cheer.

The plan worked. The mayor was furious and demanded that Benz overtake the milk wagon. Benz apologized but said that because of the ridiculous speed law he was not permitted to go any faster. Very soon after that the law was changed.

Benz proved that the art of diplomacy is getting people to see things *your* way.

~ Karl Benz

❖

An Easterner who walked into a Western saloon was amazed to see a dog sitting at a table playing poker with three men. He asked, "Can that dog really read cards?"

"Yeah, but he ain't much of a player," said one of the men. "Whenever he gets a good hand he wags his tail."

Every once in a while someone who is unprepared is given more responsibility and surprises everyone by doing an excellent job. More often, though, the person with too little training shows it immediately. It usually takes time to discover the best ways of doing things and make them a habit.

In breaking in new employees, by all means try to stay relaxed. Don't act important. Smile! If you have a sense of humor, don't be afraid to show it. It will bring some welcome sunshine into lives of the people who work for you.

A sense of humor doesn't mean the ability to tell jokes or make wisecracks. It's a sense of proportion and the courage to smile. It's the ability to smile at yourself and the world as well.

We're all in this thing together – grains of sand passing through the hourglass of time. The least we can do for each other is being as pleasant about it as possible. Why compound our miseries with ulcers?

~ John Luther

Back in the 1920s, an executive of the New York Telephone Company stopped in amazement one evening to observe a man in a tuxedo emerging from a manhole at the corner of 42nd Street and Broadway.

The man turned out to be Burch Foraker, head of the Bell telephone system in New York City. On that cold January night, Foraker had come out of a theater and descended into the manhole.

Was there a crisis? Was he worried about some serious difficulty in the system? No, it was nothing of the sort.

"I knew there were a couple of my cable splicers working down there, so I just dropped in on 'em to have a little chat," said Foraker.

In time, Foraker became known as the "man of ten thousand friends," due in part to the fact that he made a habit of visiting his men at their work. It was his way of showing that he considered their jobs important.

Good managers and executives show their associates that they respect their ability. They display a genuine interest in what they are doing. They drop in, chat a bit, ask a few questions and perhaps make a useful suggestion. Try it. It never does any harm and it can do a lot of good.

❖

If you want to manage your time better, the first step, as suggested by time management consultant, Alan Lakein, is to ask yourself this question: 'Exactly what are my goals?"

Take a blank sheet of paper. List your personal lifetime goals, the things you would like to be able to look back upon by the time you are eighty; not general things, such as to be happy, but specific goals, such as a trip to Europe, a master's degree, a savings-account balance of a specific figure, a vacation home, a specific weight loss, a working knowledge of Spanish and so on.

Now list your professional goals. Do not list such generalities as a higher salary or a promotion or greater prestige, but specific things like a salary of certain amount, promotion to a particular job, or election to a specific office in a professional society.

Then make a list of short-term goals, the things you would like to accomplish in the next six months.

Besides being specific, goals should be attainable and authentic—in other words, *things you really want and are willing to work for.* Keep in mind that they are subject to change at any time; indeed, one of your priority tasks should be to look over your list of goals and update it. But the list should represent your best judgment of what you'd like to accomplish as of this moment.

Now, analyze your lists. They probably include more things than you reasonably can expect to do, so assign priorities. Select three or four goals in each category that you consider most important and write them down some place where you will see them every day. Memorize them. And a hundred times a day, ask yourself, "Is what I am doing now moving me closer to one of my goals?" If the answer is no, figure out some way the activity can be eliminated, delegated to someone else or downgraded in priority so that it can be accomplished in your productive time.

❖

Jackie Robinson made history when he became the first black baseball player to break into the major leagues by joining the Brooklyn Dodgers.

Branch Rickey, owner of the Dodgers at that time, told Robin-son, "It'll be tough. You're going to take abuse you never dreamed of, but if you're willing to try, I'll back you all the way."

And Rickey was right. Jackie was abused verbally (not to mention physically by runners coming into second base). Racial slurs from the crowd and members of his own team, as well as from opponents, were standard fare.

One day, Robinson was having it particularly tough. He had booted two ground balls, and boos were cascading over the diamond. In full view of thousands of spectators, Pee Wee Reese, the captain and Dodger short-stop, walked over and put his arm around Jackie right in the middle of the game. "That may have saved my career," Robinson reflected later. "Pee Wee made me feel that I belonged."

Be sure that the employees on your team feel that they belong.

~ Dr. Denis Waitley
The Double Win

Barbara Boggs Sigmund wore an eye patch. She lost her eye to cancer in 1982 in the middle of her campaign for election to the U.S. Senate from New Jersey. Two days after her surgery, she was scheduled to speak at a political function.

Barbara's mother handed her a pair of spiked high heels and told her to wear them and walk up the stairs to the speaking platform. Her sister gasped. "Those were death-defying heels," she told a reporter. "Momma was of the opinion that if people saw her walk up those stairs in those shoes, they'd figure she could do anything."

Barbara wore the shoes. When her time came, she walked up the steps without hesitation and went to the podium. "You're all a sight for a sore eye," she said into the microphone. She lost that primary, but won many followers and was elected mayor of Princeton, New Jersey, the fol-lowing year.

Barbara lost her battle with cancer on October 10, 1990. She counted as her proudest achievement the founding of Womanspace, the first bat-tered women's shelter in Mercer County, New Jersey. It was used as a model for other shelters.

"When life gives you lemons," she said, "make lemonade."

Her accomplishments and will to win far outweighed any deadly disease or handicap.

❖

When you ask people to do something, be sure to also tell them why. It is well worth the time and effort.

It's very easy for a busy person to fall into the habit of simply telling people to do things without further explanation. It seems like the quickest and easiest way to get things done.

But it's rarely the best way. When you ask someone to do some-thing, take time to explain why. It's an excellent habit with a lot of good side effects.

Explaining why you want something done automatically removes the curse of "bossiness." When there's a good reason why something ought to be done, it puts you in the position of simply making a logical, reasonable request. It completely removes the bad taste that comes from "ordering people around."

When you explain why, you also lessen the chance of error. People who understand why they're doing something are less apt to foul it up. And if the situation changes – so that the action is no longer required – they'll have sense enough to stop. If they don't understand, they'll have no choice but to go blindly ahead doing what you told them to.

Explaining the reason for your request is a compliment to the people you've asked to carry it out. It shows that you think it's important that they should understand what they're doing and be able to use their heads. You also put them in a position to make suggestions – and these can be very helpful.

People aren't robots or push buttons. The more you can treat them like intelligent human beings with good brains in their heads, the better your results will be.

Sure – there are times when the reason is so obvious to everyone that it isn't worth mentioning. And there are also times of emergency when people have to do what they are told and pronto! But the general rule still stands: *when you ask someone to do something, explain why.*

❖

You don't have to be brilliant to be a good leader. But you do have to understand other people – how they feel, what makes them tick, and the best way to influence them.

There are a lot of brilliant people in this world who are, and will remain, ineffective leaders. Why? It is because they are so interested in themselves and their own accomplishments that they never get around to appreciating and understanding the feelings of the other people who are sharing this world with them.

Sometimes, usually later in life, these talented, egocentric individuals suffer painful hardships. They understand, often for the first time, the kinds of problems others are facing. If they would have made an effort and tried to put themselves in other people's shoes, or tried to imagine how they might feel if they were in the same circumstance, then they would have been aware of what makes others tick, and would have tried to be helpful, and at the same time, would have received help from others.

~ John Luther

❖

In 1951, 24-year old Lillian Katz wanted to add $50.00 to her husband's weekly income of $75.00. Pregnant with their first son, she took $2,000.00 of wedding gift money, bought some supplies, and sent $500.00 to *Seventeen* magazine to place an ad for personalized hand-bags and belts to be sold by mail. "Be the first to sport that personalized look," read the ad. "Personalizing" involved putting the customer's initial on a handbag or belt.

"I figured that for $125.00 a week we could do everything we wanted," she recalls. "I liked the stimulation of work, and I wasn't prepared to do only child care. I chose the mail order business simply because it was the only thing I could think of that would allow me to work at home and be with my children."

Within six weeks after the first ad appeared, Lillian Katz was at her kitchen table sorting through $16,000.00 worth of orders.

Today the Lillian Vernon Corporation has annual sales of $137 million. Her company receives 30,000 telephone orders weekly and employs 1,000 people.

❖

When Calvin Coolidge was Vice President, Channing Cox who had suc-ceeded Coolidge as Governor of Massachusetts, came to Washington and stopped in to see him. Cox was impressed by the fact that Coolidge was able to see long lists of callers every day, yet finished his work by five o'clock. Cox pointed out that he often found himself tied up with visitors until nine in the evening. "What makes the difference?" he asked.

"You talk back," silent Cal explained.

❖

Lateness and absenteeism are two of industry's biggest problems. An-yone who knew a sure cure for them could sell the secret and retire in luxury.

It's hard enough to schedule work efficiently even when everyone shows up. And when people are unexpectedly late or absent, adjust-ments have to be made at the last minute. These makeshift changes are usually costly and inefficient.

There is, of course, no final solution. Like death and taxes, lateness and absenteeism will always be with us. Nevertheless, there are things a supervisor can do to minimize the problem.

One is to be sure, through personal contact and explanation, that eve-ryone appreciates the problems that lateness and absenteeism create. Some people believe it's nobody's business but their own. They must be helped to see that their actions affect the entire group, that they are part of a team. When they're late or absent, they're letting the others down.

❖

When Casey Stengel was seventy years old, the Yankees unceremo-niously dumped him as manager five days after the 1960 World Series. New York had lost the series by the narrowest of margins when a Pitts-burgh player dramatically homered in the bottom of the ninth inning of the seventh and deciding game. Up to that fateful moment, Stengel had won seven World Series and ten American League pennants in twelve years as Yankee manager, a record that no one has surpassed.

"I've been fired because of my age," Stengel said. "I'll never make the mistake of being seventy again."

Lincoln attributed his excellent memory to a lifelong habit of reading out loud. 'When I read aloud two senses catch the idea. First, I see what I read. Second, I hear it and, therefore, I can remember it better."

Have you ever received a letter from a highly successful, prominent business executive? We get such letters, on rare occasions, and we've noticed that, in some respects at least, they are very similar.

They are usually brief, sometimes no more than two or three sentences.

They don't waste time on contrived introductory remarks or lengthy conclusions.

They get immediately to the point, say what has to be said in the simplest possible fashion, and then sign off.

Why should such prominent, highly successful people be so thrifty with words? We suspect it's because they no longer feel any need to try to impress people. Perhaps some of them never did. In the midst of today's wordiness and huffing and puffing, their letters are a breath of fresh air.

When the Rivera United Methodist Church in Redondo Beach, California, needed more money than the Sunday collections were bringing in, the Reverend Orlie White remembered the biblical parable of the talents. Putting that parable into practice, Rev. White filled a collection plate with ten-dollar bills and invited each of his 200 parishioners to take one. He asked them to use the money to try to make more money, then to return the original ten dollars and the amount it had earned to the church.

One woman bought needles and yarn and crocheted covers for clothes hangers, which she sold for a profit of $38.00. Another used the money to enter a bowling tournament and won a $75.00 prize for the church. A man and his wife pooled their stake and bought a share of stock for $20.00. Three months later they sold it for more than $50.00.

By the end of the year, the original $2,000 had grown into $8,000.

A professor in Switzerland warned her class to beware of polls and pollsters. "They can get any answer they want with loaded questions," she warned. She cited the case of Swiss voters who replied "no" when asked if they approved of smoking while praying. "The vote turned to 'yes' when the same people were asked if they approved of praying while smoking," she told her class.

Albert Einstein always had a wholesome disregard for the tyranny of custom. Once, as the guest of honor at a dinner party given for him by the president of Swarthmore College, he was called on for a speech.

"Ladies and gentlemen" he said, "I am sorry, but I have nothing to say," and sat down. Then he arose and added, "In case I do have something to say, I'll come back."

Six months later he wired the president, "Now I have something to say." Another dinner was held and Einstein made his speech.

The president of a successful company was asked what it took to get to the top. "The same thing it took to get started," he replied, "a sense of urgency about getting things done."

The people who make things move in this world share this same sense of urgency.

No matter how intelligent or able you may be, if you don't have this sense of urgency, now is the time to start developing it. The world is full of very competent people who honestly intend to do things tomorrow, or as soon as they can get around to it. Their accomplishments, however, seldom match those of less talented people who are blessed with a sense of importance of getting started now.

Frank Lloyd Wright is among the most innovative architects this country ever produced. But his fame wasn't limited to the United States. About

70 years ago, Japan asked Wright to design a hotel for Tokyo that would be capable of surviving an earthquake.

When the architect visited Japan to see where the Imperial Hotel was to be built, he was appalled to find only about eight feet of earth on the site. Beneath that was 60 feet of mud that slipped and shook like jelly. Every test hole he dug filled up immediately with water. A lesser man probably would have given up right there, but not Frank Lloyd Wright.

Since the hotel was going to rest on fluid ground, Wright decided to build it like a ship. Instead of trying to keep the structure from moving during a quake, he incorporated features that would allow the hotel to ride out the shock without damage. Supports were sunk into the soft mud, and sections of the foundation were cantilevered from the supports. The rooms were built in sections like a train and hinged together. Water pipes and electric lines, usually the first to shear off in an earthquake, were hung in vertical shafts where they could sway freely if necessary.

Wright knew that the major cause of destruction after an earthquake was fire, because water lines are apt to be broken in the ground and there is no way to put the fire out. So he insisted on a large outdoor pool in the courtyard of his hotel, "Just in case."

On September 1, 1923, Tokyo had the greatest earthquake in its history. There were fires all over the city, and 140,000 people died. Back in the U.S., news reports were slow coming in. One newspaper wanted to print the story that the Imperial Hotel had been destroyed, as rumor had it. But when a reporter called Frank Lloyd Wright, he said that they could print the story if they wished, but they would only have to retract it later. He knew the hotel would not collapse.

Shortly afterward, Wright got a telegram from Japan. The Imperial Hotel was completely undamaged. Not only that; it had provided a home for hundreds of displaced people. And when fires that raged all around the hotel threatened to spread, bucket brigades kept the structure wetted down with water from the hotel's pool.

The Imperial Hotel isn't there anymore. It was finally torn down in the 1960's to be replaced by a more modern structure.

❖

During periods of great change, answers don't last very long but a *question* is worth a lot. The question is derived from the Latin 'queaerere' (to seek), which means the same root as the word *quest.* A creative life is a continued quest, and good questions are useful guides. We have found that the most useful questions are open-minded; they allow a fresh, unanticipated answer to reveal itself.

These are the kinds of questions children aren't afraid to ask. They seem naïve at first, but think how different our lives would be if certain questions of wonder were never asked. Jim Collins of Stanford's Graduate School of Business has compiled the following list of questions of wonder:

What would a light wave look like to someone keeping pace with it?
~ Albert Einstein

What happens if I pour rubber into my waffle iron?
~ Bill Bowerman: (inventor of Nike shoes)

Why can't there be reliable overnight mail service?
~ Fred Smith (founder of Federal Express)

Why can't we see in three dimensions what is inside a human body without cutting it open?
~ Godfrey Hounsfield (inventor of the CAT scanner)
Why don't we remove the recording function and speaker and put headphones in the recorder? (Result the Sony Walkman)
~ Masaru Ibuka (Honorary Chairman, Sony)

Many of these questions were deemed ridiculous at first. Other shoe companies thought Bowerman's waffle shoe was a "really stupid idea." Godfrey Hounsfield was told the CAT scan was "impractical." Masaru Ibuka got comments like, "A recorder with no speaker and no recorder - are you crazy?" Fred Smith proposed the idea of Federal Express in a paper at Yale and got a C.

Here's a simple exercise you can do to develop your ability to ask questions that can produce radically new and unexpected ideas. Each day, for a week, take a few minutes to ask yourself a question that begins: "I wonder. . ." Ask this question about a particular area of your life, such as the workplace. "I wonder what would happen if we divided the corporations into twelve smaller, autonomous companies!" It is essential not to censor yourself, no matter how impractical or outlandish the question sounds.

After you have had some practice doing this try going public with your questions by posing them to friends or colleagues. Focus on something you are sincerely curious about and that matters to others. Listen carefully to their responses. As in the story of the Emperor's New Clothes, you'll probably discover that your question reveals blind spots and assumptions that deserve to be challenged.

❖

Leo Tolstoy once wrote a story about a successful peasant farmer who was not satisfied with his lot. He wanted more of everything.

One day he received a novel offer. For 1,000 rubles, he could buy all the land he could walk around in a day. The only catch in the deal was that he had to be back at his starting point by sundown.

Early the next morning he started out walking at a fast pace. By midday he was very tired, but he kept going, covering more and more ground. Well into the afternoon he realized that his greed had taken him far from the starting point. He quickened his pace and as the sun began to sink low in the sky, he began to run knowing that if he did not make it back by sundown the opportunity to become an ever bigger landholder would be lost.

As the sun began to sink below the horizon he came within sight of the finish line. Gasping for breath, his heart pounding, he called upon every bit of strength left in his body and staggered across the line just before the sun disappeared. He immediately collapsed, blood streaming from his mouth. In a few minutes he was dead.

Afterwards, his servants dug a grave. It was not much over six feet long and three feet wide.

The title of Tolstoy's story was: *How Much Land Does a Man Need?*

❖

An Indian and two cowboys had ridden hard since daylight. Toward evening, the cowboys talked hungrily about the big meals they would eat when they got to town. When one of them asked the Indian if he was hungry, however, he shrugged and said, "No."

Finally arriving at their destination, the three ordered steaks with all the trimmings. As the Indian proceeded to wolf down everything in sight, one of his friends reminded him that less than an hour ago he had told him he wasn't hungry.

"Not wise to be hungry then," he replied. "No food."

A construction crew was building a new road through a rural area, knocking down trees as it progressed.

A superintendent noticed that one tree had a nest of birds that couldn't yet fly and he marked the tree so that it would not be cut down.

Several weeks later the superintendent came back to the tree. He got into a bucket truck and was lifted up so that he could peer into the nest. The fledglings were gone. They had obviously learned to fly. The superintendent ordered the tree cut down.

As the tree crashed to the ground, the nest fell clear and some of the material that the birds had gathered to make the nest was scattered about. Part of it was a scrap torn from a Sunday school pamphlet. On the scrap of paper were these words: *He careth for you.*

He was born in 1735 in Massachusetts. Every student knows his name and can recite the illustrious deed he performed in 1775 during the Revolution. What is not so well known is that he was one of the world's great metal craftsmen and artisans, a pioneer manufacturer and industrialist. In 1801, he founded a major American company that is still alive and thriving today. The company is Revere Copper and Brass, Inc. and the founder was, of course, Paul Revere.

Here's a young girl who is destined to succeed. She visited a farm one day and wanted to buy a large watermelon. "That's three dollars," said the farmer. "I've only got 30 cents," said the young girl. The farmer pointed to a very small watermelon in the field and said, "How about that one?"

"Okay, I'll take it," said the little girl, handing him the money, "but leave it on the vine. I'll be back for it in a month."

Many men have written creeds, those principles by which they live and in which they believe. One of the finest is this one by John D. Rockefeller, Jr. It is familiar to many people, but is so good that it should be reread at least once a year.

I believe in the supreme worth of the individual and in his right to life, liberty and pursuit of happiness.

I believe that every right implies a responsibility; every opportunity, an obligation; every possession, a duty.

I believe that the law was made for man and not man for the law, that government is the servant of the people and not their master.

I believe in the dignity of labor, whether with head or hand; that the world owes no man a living, but that it owes every man an opportunity to make a living.

I believe that thrift is essential to well-ordered living and that economy is a prime requisite of a sound financial structure, whether in government, business, or personal affairs.

I believe that truth and justice are fundamental to an enduring social order.

I believe in the sacredness of a promise, that a man's word should be as good as his bond; that character, not wealth or power or position, is of supreme worth.

I believe that the rendering of useful service is the common duty of mankind and that only in the purifying fire of sacrifice is the dross of self-ishness consumed and the greatness of the human soul set free.

I believe in an all-wise and all-loving GOD, named by whatever name, and that the individual's highest fulfillment, greatest happiness, and wisest usefulness are to be found in living in harmony with His will.

I believe that love is the greatest thing in the world; that it alone can overcome hate; that right can and will triumph over wrong.

❖

Most creative people are not happy unless they are trying to solve a problem. They can't look at anything without wondering how it might be changed, improved, adapted, modified, or otherwise tinkered with.

Charles F. Kettering, the inventor who contributed so much into the auto industry, was that kind of man. He compared this kind of creative thinking with hanging bird cages in the mind.

Kettering once bet a friend that if he were given a bird cage and hung it up in his house, then the friend would sooner or later have to buy a bird. The friend took the bet.

"I got him an attractive bird cage made in Switzerland," said Kettering, "and my friend hung it near his dining room table. Of course, you know what happened! People would come in and say, 'Joe, when did your bird die?' 'I never had a bird,' Joe would say. 'Well, what have you got a bird cage for?'" people would ask. Finally, my friend Joe said it was simpler to buy a bird than to keep explaining why he had an empty bird cage.

"If you hang bird cages in your mind," said Kettering, "eventually you get something to put into them."

❖

Today, if you believe some people, loyalty is dead. The relationship between an employee and his or her company is strictly a matter of, "What have you done for me lately?" Nothing matters except a dollar in the pocket right now—today.

But is this really true? Have people really changed that much? Or does this view merely reflect the frustrations of those managers who haven't bothered to develop the warm, direct, person-to-person relationships with their associates that lead to loyalty?

It's true that employees aren't as indiscriminately loyal as they used to be. Today's workers take a lot more convincing that you really have their interest at heart—not just your own. But it can still be done. Supervisors or managers who work at it can still develop a feeling of loyalty among their people.

The key to loyalty is deserving it—and showing that you do. What kind of leaders deserve loyalty? Among other things, they're people. . .

Who give loyalty

Who are sincerely and genuinely interested in the present and future of those who work for them

Who appreciate their viewpoints, problems, hopes and ambitions

Who deal with them openly, honestly, and fairly

Who delegate responsibility and develop people

Who give and share credit liberally.

It takes all this, sometimes more, to earn loyalty. Perhaps that's why more managers complain about the lack of loyalty that truly deserves it. But it can be had; it's well worth the price.

At the age of forty-two, George Sand, the famous nineteenth century French novelist, was a broken and depressed human being. (She had adopted the male pseudonym to cover the fact that her novels were written by a woman.)

Her personal life at this time had fallen apart and she was the victim of severe personal criticism from powerful and influential people in France.

One day, feeling low and melancholy, she wandered into the woods near her home where she had played as a child. Seated there on a boulder she thought over the past, pondered her future, and tried to analyze her personal situation. After some time she reached a conclusion that was to enable her to go on and write another 50 plays and novels. That decision was this:

"Henceforth I shall accept what I am and what I am not. With my limitations and my gifs, I shall go on using life as long as I am in this world and afterwards. Not to use life—that alone is death."

Two gardeners for wealthy estates on Long Island met one day at the local hardware store. "I hear you're working for that banker fellow," said one.

"You've got it all wrong," replied the other. "He gets up at five-thirty every morning to get aboard an overcrowded, rickety train to commute to the hot city so he can keep up his estate and pay us all weekly wages. No, I'm not working for him; he's working for me!"

❖

Motivational speaker Bill Gove tells a story about Harry, who ran a small appliance store in Phoenix, Arizona.

Harry was used to price-shopping by young couples. They would ask detailed questions about features, prices and model numbers, and one of them always took notes. Harry knew that as soon as they left the store they were going to head for one of the discount appliance dealers to make comparisons. Nevertheless, Harry would patiently answer all their questions, even though it took more than a half hour at times. But when the couple would announce that they were going to look around at some other places, Harry had a standard spiel to deliver.

"I know that you're looking for the best deal you can find," he would say. "I understand that, because I do the same thing myself. I know you'll probably go to Discount Dan's to compare prices. I know I would.

"But after you've done that, I want you to think of one thing. When you buy from Discount Dan's, you get an appliance—a good one, I know, because he sells the same appliances we do. But when you buy here, you get one thing you don't get at Dan's. You get me. I come with the deal. I stand behind what I sell. I want you to be happy with what you buy. I've been here 30 years. I learned the business from my Dad, and I hope to be able to give the business over to my daughter and son-in-law in a few years.

"So you know one thing for sure—when you buy any appliance from me, you get me with the deal. That means I'll do everything I can to be sure you never regret doing business with me. That's a guarantee."

Harry would then wish the couple well and give them a quart of ice cream in appreciation of their stopping at his store.

This is how Bill Gove finished the story: "Now", he says, "how far do you think that couple is going to get, with Harry's speech ringing in their ears and a quart of ice cream on their hands in Phoenix when it's 110 degrees in the shade?"

❖

There is an ancient tale about a king who wanted to pick the wisest man among his subjects to be his prime minister. When the search finally narrowed down to three men, he decided to put them to the supreme test. Accordingly, he placed them together in a room in his palace. On the room door he installed a lock that was the last word in mechanical ingenuity. The candidates were informed that whoever was able to open the door first would be appointed to the post of honor.

The three men immediately set themselves to the task. Two of them began at once to work out complicated mathematical formulas to discover the proper lock combinations. The third man, however, just sat down in his chair, lost in thought. Finally, without bothering to put pen to paper, he got up, walked to the door, and turned the handle. The door opened to his touch. It had been unlocked all the time!

In his book, *Tough-Minded Leadership,* management consultant Joe Batten reproduces a pledge—a rededication to excellence in leadership that managers of the Marriott Corporation sign each year.

Batten first became aware of the pledge in 1972 during a meeting with J. Willard (Bill) Marriott Sr., founder of the hotel and restaurant chain, and his son Bill Marriott Jr., the current chief executive. During the meeting, Batten asked the Marriotts what the key to their success was. Both pointed to the Marriott Pledge as the most important factor. They said that performance standards, performance appraisals, compensation reviews, promotions, and all key administrative decisions had to be demonstrably based on the pledge. Each year, all members of Marriott management receive a copy of the pledge. They sign it, send it back to headquarters, and it goes into their personnel file.

Before Batten left the meeting, he was given a copy of the pledge. Here it is:

I promise the members of my team:
To set the right example for them by my own actions in all things.
To be consistent in my temperament so that they know how to "read" me and what to expect from me.
To be fair, impartial, and consistent in matters relating to work rules, discipline, and rewards.

To show a sincere, personal interest in them as individuals without becoming overly "familiar."

To seek their counsel on matters that affect their jobs and to be guided as much as possible by their judgment.

To allow them as much individuality as possible in the way their jobs are performed, as long as the quality of the end result is not compromised.

To make sure they always know in advance what I expect from them in the way of conduct and performance on the job.

To be appreciative of their efforts and generous in praise of their accomplishments.

To use every opportunity to teach them how to do their jobs better and how to help themselves advance in skill level and responsibility.

To show them that I can "do" as well as "manage" by pitching in to work beside them.

Signed: _____

❖

Never Judge a Book by its Cover

A lady in a faded gingham dress and her husband, dressed in a homespun threadbare suit, stepped off the train in Boston and walked timidly without an appointment into the Harvard University President's outer office. The secretary could tell in a moment that such backwoods, country hicks had no business at Harvard and probably didn't even deserve to be in Cambridge.

"We'd like to see the president," the man said softly.

"He'll be busy all day," the secretary snapped.

"We'll wait," the lady replied.

For hours the secretary ignored them, hoping that the couple would finally become discouraged and go away. They didn't, and the secretary grew frustrated and finally decided to disturb the president, even though it was a chore she always regretted. "Maybe if you see them for a few minutes, they'll leave," she said to him. He sighed in exasperation and nodded. Someone of his importance obviously didn't have the time to spend with them, and he detested gingham dresses and homespun suits cluttering up his outer office.

The president, stern faced and with dignity, strutted toward the couple. The woman told him, "We had a son who attended Harvard for one year. He loved Harvard. He was happy here. However, about a year ago, he was accidentally killed. My husband and I would like to erect a memorial to him somewhere on campus."

The president wasn't touched. He was shocked. "Madam," he said, gruffly, "we can't put up a statue for every person who attended Harvard and died. If we did, this place would look like a cemetery."

"Oh, no," the lady explained quickly. "We don't want to erect a statue. We thought we would like to give a building to Harvard."

The president rolled his eyes. He glanced at the gingham dress and homespun suit, and then exclaimed, "A building! Do you have any earthly idea how much a building costs? We have over seven and a half million dollars in the physical buildings here at Harvard."

For a moment, the lady was silent. The president was pleased. Maybe he could get rid of them now. The lady turned to her husband and said quietly, "Is that all it costs to start a university? Why don't we just start our own?" Her husband nodded.

The president's face wilted in confusion and bewilderment. Mr. and Mrs. Leland Stanford got up and walked away, traveling to Palo Alto, California, where they established the university that bears their name, Stanford University, a memorial to a son that Harvard no longer cared about. You can easily judge the character of others by how they treat those who they think can do nothing for them.

A True Story, written by Malcolm Forbes

"People will forget what you said. People will forget what you did. But people will never forget how you made them feel!"

The late Dr. Maxwell Maltz once traveled to Lake Orion, near Detroit, to talk to a group of priests who had succumbed to alcoholism.

"They came from all over the world and were treated for four months," said Dr. Maltz, "then returned to their flocks cured. During their treatment, they used my book Psycho-Cybernetics (Pocket Books, Simon and Schuster) as a bridge to get back to themselves."

After lecturing I went to sleep for a few hours. I was awakened at 1:45 a.m. Lake Orion is about forty-five miles from Detroit, and I had to catch the 4:35 a.m. plane back to New York so that I could operate on a child who had been seriously injured in an automobile accident."

The night man, after waking me, took me to the main house of the priest's sanitarium and made me scrambled eggs and coffee. This simple action touched me because it was not his job, and I had not asked him to make a meal for me. He stood there, bushy hair, rosy cheeks and asked me if the eggs were okay."

"'Fine," I said, and thanked him for putting himself out for me at 2:00a.m.

"I just wanted to help," he said, and gave me a shy, friendly smile.

After some small talk, he told me about himself. He had a bad heart. Under his shirt he wore a pacemaker, an electrical instrument attached to the chest wall. The instrument helped him keep his heart beating normally, enabling him to live and work as night man at the sanitarium."

"Another cup of coffee?" he asked. I nodded.

"I like to help," he said. "I really do. Since I had my heart trouble, especially. I live a good life. I like to help people, and I take other people's help. I've got no complaints."

On the plane from Detroit to New York, I thought about this man who lived a simple life and enjoyed it. I said to myself, "If a man who can't live without an electrical instrument will not give in, we can all learn the lesson that, despite our problems, we can stand up to the stresses of the day and refuse to withdraw our strength. By activating our success mechanism, every day, we can live each day to the full."

❖

You Can't Fix Stupid

These people prove stupid is a terminal condition. As always, competition this year has been keen. The candidates this year are. . .

8th place:

In Detroit, a 41-year-old man got stuck and drowned in two feet of water after squeezing head first through an 18-inch wide sewer grate to retrieve his car keys.

7th place:

A 49-year-old San Francisco stockbroker, who totally 'zoned' when he ran, accidentally jogged off a 100-foot high cliff on his daily run.

6th place:

While at the beach, Daniel Jones, 21, dug an 8-foot hole for protection from the wind. He was sitting in a beach chair at the bottom of it when it collapsed, burying him beneath five feet of sand. People on the beach used their hands and shovels trying to get him out but could not reach him. It took rescue workers using heavy equipment almost an hour to free him. Jones was pronounced dead at the hospital.

5th place:

Santiago Alvarado, 24, was killed as he fell through the ceiling of a bicycle shop he was burglarizing. Death was caused when the long flashlight he had placed in his mouth to keep his hands free rammed into the base of his skull as he hit the floor.

4th place:

Sylvester Briddell, Jr., 26, was killed as he won a bet with friends who said he would not put a revolver loaded with four bullets into his mouth and pull the trigger.

3rd place:

After stepping around a marked police car parked at the front door, a man walked into H&J Leather & Firearms intent on robbing the store. The shop was full of customers and a uniformed officer was standing at the counter. Upon seeing the officer, the would-be robber announced a hold-up, and fired a few wild shots from a target pistol. The officer and a clerk promptly returned fire, and several customers also drew their guns and fired. The robber was pronounced dead at the scene by paramedics. Crime scene investigators located 47 expended cartridge cases in the shop. The subsequent autopsy revealed 23 gunshot wounds. Ballistics identified rounds from 7 different weapons. No one else was hurt.

Honorable Mention:

Paul Stiller, 47, and his wife Bonnie were bored just driving around at 2:00 a.m. They lit a quarter stick of dynamite to toss out the window to see what would happen. Apparently they failed to notice the window was closed.

Runner Up:

Kerry Bingham had been drinking with several friends when one of them said they knew a person who had bungee-jumped from a local bridge in the middle of traffic. The conversation grew more heated and at least 10 men trooped along the walkway of the bridge at 4:30 a.m.
    Upon arrival at the midpoint of the bridge they discovered that no one had brought a bungee rope. Bingham, who had continued drinking, volunteered and pointed out that a coil of lineman's cable lay nearby. They secured one end around Bingham's leg and then tied the other to the bridge. His fall lasted 40 feet before the cable tightened and tore his foot off at the ankle. He miraculously survived his fall into the icy water and was rescued by two nearby fishermen. Bingham's foot was never located.

AND THE WINNER IS:

Zookeeper, Friedrich Riesfeldt, (Padeborn, Germany) fed his consti-pated elephant 22 doses of animal laxative and more than a bushel of berries, figs and prunes before the plugged-up pachyderm finally got relief. Investigators say ill-fated Friedrich, 46, was attempting to give the ailing elephant an olive oil enema when the relieved beast unloaded. The sheer force of the elephant's unexpected defecation knocked Mr. Riesfeldt to the ground where he struck his head on a rock as the elephant continued to evacuate some 200 pounds of dung on top of him. It seems to be just one of those freak accidents that proves: 'Shit happens'.

In 1784, Benjamin Franklin, wrote the following letter to a man named Benjamin Webb:

Dear Sir:

Your situation grieves me and I send you herewith a banknote for ten louis d'or. I do not pretend to give such a sum; I only lend it to you. When you shall return to your country, you cannot fail of getting into some business that will enable you to pay all your debts.

In that case, when you meet with another honest man in similar distress, you must pay me by lending the sum to him, enjoining him to discharge the debt by a like operation when he shall be able and shall meet with such another opportunity.

I hope it may thus go through many hands before it meets with a knave that will stop its progress. This is a trick of mine for doing a deal of good with a little money. I am not rich enough to afford much in good works, and so am obliged to be cunning and make the most of a little.

With best wishes for your future prosperity, I am, dear sir, your most obedient servant.

B. Franklin

You know me, I'm a nice person. When I get lousy service, I never complain. I never kick, I never criticize and I wouldn't dream of making a scene.

I'm one of those nice customers. And I'll tell you what else I am. I'm the customer who doesn't come back. I take whatever you hand out, because I know I am not coming back. I could tell you off and feel better, but in the long run, it's better to just leave quietly.

You see, a nice customer like me, multiplied by others like me, can, bring a business to its knees. There are plenty of us. When we get pushed far enough, we go to one of your competitors.

❖

A friend's grandfather came to America from Europe and after being processed at Ellis Island, he went into a cafeteria in New York City to get something to eat. He sat down at an empty table and waited for someone to take his order. Of course, nobody ever did. Finally, a man with a tray full of food sat down opposite him and told him how things worked.

"Start at that end," he said, "and just go along and pick out what you want. At the other end they'll tell you how much you have to pay for it."

"I soon learned that's how everything works in America," Grandpa told our friend. "Life is a cafeteria here. You can get anything you want as long as you're willing to pay the price. You can even get success. But you'll never get it if you wait for someone to bring it to you. You have to get up and get it yourself."

VIII

Reflections of Me, Myself and I

For it isn't your father, mother, friends, coach, wife, boss, teacher, or siblings,

Whose judgment on you must pass.

The person's whose verdict counts most in your life,

Is the one staring back from the glass.

The Man in the Glass

When you get what you want in your struggle thru life
And the world makes you king for a day
Just go to a mirror and look at yourself
And see what that man has to say

For it isn't your father, mother, coach or wife
Whose judgment on you must pass
The fellow whose verdict counts most in your life
Is the one staring back from the glass

You may be like Jack Horner and chisel a plum
And think you're a wonderful guy
But the man in the glass says you're only a bum
If you can't look him straight in the eye

He's the fellow to please, never mind all the rest
For he's with you right up to the end
And you've passed your most dangerous difficult test
If the man in the glass is your friend

You may fool the entire world down thru the years
And get pats on the back as you pass
But your final reward will be heartaches and tears
If you've cheated – The Man in the Glass

Our business in life is not to get ahead of others, but to get ahead of ourselves—to break our own records, to outstrip our yesterday with our today.

~ Stewart B. Johnson

Decision 1 – The Responsible Decision

The Buck Stops Here!

From this moment forward, I will accept responsibility for my past. I understand that the beginning of wisdom is to accept the responsibility for my own problems and that by accepting responsibility for my past. I free myself to move into a bigger, brighter future of my own choosing.

Never again will I blame my parents, my spouse, my boss, or employees for my present situation. Neither my education of lack of one, my genetics, or the circumstantial ebb and flow of everyday life will affect my future in a negative way. If I allow myself to blame these uncontrollable forces for my lack of success, I will be forever caught in a web of the past. I will look forward. I will not let my history control my destiny.

The buck stops here. I accept responsibility for my past. I am responsible for my success. I am where I am today—mentally, physically, spiritually, emotionally, and financially—because of decisions I have made. My decisions have always been governed by my thinking. Therefore, I am where I am today—because of how I think. Today I will begin the process of changing where I am—mentally, physically, spiritually, emotionally, and financially—by changing the way I think

My thoughts will be constructive, never destructive. My mind will live in the solutions of the future. It will not dwell in the problems of the past. I will seek the association of those who are working and striving to bring about positive changes in the world. I will never seek comfort by associating with those who have decided to be comfortable.

When faced with the opportunity to make a decision, I will make one. I understand that God did not put in me the ability to always make right decisions. He did, however, put in me the ability to make a decision and then make it right. The rise and fall of my emotional tide will not deter me from my course. When I make a decision, I will stand behind it. My energy will go into making the decision. I will waste none on second thoughts. My life will not be an apology. It will be a statement.

The buck stops here. I control my thoughts. I control my emotions.

In the future, when I am tempted to ask the question, "Why me?" I will immediately counter with the answer: "Why not me?" Challenges are a gift, an opportunity to learn. Problems are the common thread running through the lives of great men and women. In times of adversity, I will not have a problem to deal with, I will have a choice to make. My thoughts will be clear. I will make the right choice. Adversity is preparation for greatness. I will accept the preparation. Why me? Why not me? I will be prepared for something great!

I accept responsibility for my past. I control my thoughts. I control my emotions. I am responsible for my success.

~ Andy Andrews

Decision 2 — The Guided Decision

I will seek wisdom!

Knowing that wisdom waits to be gathered, I will actively search her out. My past can never be changed, but I can change the future by changing my actions today. I will change my actions today! I will train my eyes and ears to read and listen to books and recordings that bring about positive changes in my personal relationships and a greater understanding of my fellow man. No longer will I bombard my mind with materials that feed my doubts and fears. I will read and listen only to that which increases my belief in myself and my future.

I will seek wisdom. I will choose my friends with care. I am who my friends are. I speak their language, and I wear their clothes. I share their opinions and their habits. From this moment forward, I will choose to associate with people whose lives and lifestyles I admire. If I associate with chickens, I will learn to scratch at the ground and squabble over crumbs. If I associate with eagles, I will learn to soar great heights. I am an eagle. It is my destiny to fly.

I will seek wisdom. I will listen to the counsel of wise men. The words of a wise man are like raindrops on dry ground. They are precious and quickly used for immediate results. Only the blade of grass that catches a raindrop will prosper and grow. The person who ignores wise counsel is like the blade of grass untouched by the rain—soon to wither and die. When I counsel with myself, I can only make decisions according to what I already know. By counseling with a wise man, I add his knowledge and experience to my own and dramatically increase my success.

I will seek wisdom. I will be a servant to others. A wise man will cultivate a servant's spirit, for that particular attribute attracts people like no other. As I humbly serve others, their wisdom will be freely shared with me. Often, the person who develops a servant's spirit becomes wealthy beyond measure. Many times, a servant has the ear of the king, and a humble servant becomes king for he is the popular choice of the people. He who serves the most grows the fastest.

I will become a humble servant. I will not look for someone to open my door—I will look to open the door for someone. I will not be distressed when no one is available to help me—I will be excited when I am available to help.

I will be a servant to others. I will listen to the counsel of wise men. I will choose my friends with care.

~ Andy Andrews

Decision 3 — The Active Decision

I am a person of action!

Beginning today, I will create a new future by creating a new me. No longer will I dwell in a pit of despair, moaning over squandered time and lost opportunity. I can do nothing about the past. My future is immediate. I will grasp it in both hands and carry it with running feet. When I am faced with the choice of doing nothing or doing something, I will always choose to act! I seize this moment. I choose now.

I am a person of action. I am energetic. I move quickly. Knowing that laziness is a sin, I will create a habit of lively behavior. I will walk with a spring in my step and a smile on my face. The lifeblood rushing through my veins is urging me upward and forward into activity and accomplishment. Wealth and prosperity hide from the sluggard, but rich rewards come to the person who moves quickly.

I am a person of action. I inspire others with my activity. I am a leader. Leading is doing. To lead, I must move forward. Many people move out of the way for a person on the run; others are caught up in his wake. My activity will create a wave of success for the people who follow. My activity will be consistent. This will instill confidence in my leadership. As a leader, I have the ability to encourage and inspire others to greatness. It is true.

An army of sheep led by a lion would defeat an army of lions led by a sheep!

I am a person of action. I can make a decision. I can make it now. A person who moves neither left nor right is destined for mediocrity. When faced with a decision, many people say they are waiting for God. But I understand, in most cases, God is waiting for me! He has given me a healthy mind to gather and sort information and the courage to come to a conclusion. I am not a quivering dog, indecisive and fearful. My constitution is strong and my pathway clear. Successful people make their decisions quickly and change their mind slowly. Failures make their decisions slowly and change their mind quickly. My decisions come quickly, and they lead to victory.

I am a person of action. I am daring. I am courageous. Fear no longer has a place in my life. For too long, fear has outweighed my desire to make things better for my family. Never again! I have exposed fear as a vapor, an impostor who never had any power over me in the first place! I do not fear opinion, gossip, or the idle chatter of monkeys for all are the same to me. I do not fear failure, for in my life, failure is a myth. Failure only exists for the person who quits. I do not quit.

I am courageous. I am a leader. I seize this moment. I choose now.

~ Andy Andrews

Decision 4 — The Certain Decision

I have a decided heart!

A wise man once said, "A journey of a thousand miles begins with a single step." Knowing this to be true, I am taking my first step today. For too long my feet have been tentative, shuffling left and right, more backward than forward as my heart gauged the direction of the wind. Criticism, condemnation, and complaint are creatures of the wind. They come and go on the wasted breath of lesser beings and have no power over me. The power to control direction belongs to me. Today I will begin to exercise that power. My course has been charted. My destiny is assured.

I have a decided heart. I am passionate about my vision for the future. I will awaken every morning with an excitement about the new day and its opportunity for growth and change. My thoughts and actions will work in a forward motion, never sliding into the dark forest of doubt or the muddy quicksand of self-pity. I will freely give my vision for the future to others, and as they see the belief in my eyes, they will follow me.

I will lay my head on my pillow at night happily exhausted, knowing that I have done everything within my power to move the mountains in my path. As I sleep, the same dream that dominates my waking hours will be with me in the dark. Yes, I have a dream. It is a great dream, and I will never apologize for it. Neither will I ever let it go, for if I did, my life would be finished. My hopes, my passions, my vision for the future is my very existence. A person without a dream never had a dream come true.

I have a decided heart. I will not wait.

I know that the purpose of analysis is to come to a conclusion. I have tested the angles. I have measured the probabilities. And now I have made a decision with my heart. I am not timid. I will move now and not look back. What I put off until tomorrow, I will put off until the next day as well. I do not procrastinate. All my problems become smaller when I confront them. If I touch a thistle with caution, it will prick me, but if I grasp it boldly, its spines crumble into dust.

I will not wait. I am passionate about my vision for the future. My course has been charted. My destiny is assured.

~ Andy Andrews

Decision 5 — The Joyful Decision

Today, I will choose to be happy!

Beginning this very moment, I am a happy person, for I now truly understand the concept of happiness. Few others before me have been able to grasp the truth of the physical law that enables one to live happily every day. I know now that happiness is not an emotional phantom floating in and out of my life. Happiness is a choice. Happiness is the end result of certain thoughts and activities, which actually bring about a chemical reaction in my body. This reaction results in a euphoria, which, while elusive to some, is totally under my control.

Today I will choose to be happy. I will greet each day with laughter. Within moments of awakening, I will laugh for seven seconds. After even such a small period of time, excitement has begun to flow through my bloodstream. I feel different. I am different! I am enthusiastic about the day. I am alert to its possibilities. I am happy! Laughter is an outward expression of enthusiasm, and I know that enthusiasm is the fuel that moves the world. I laugh throughout the day. I laugh while I am alone, and I laugh in conversation with others. People are drawn to me because I have laughter in my heart. The world belongs to the enthusiastic for people will follow them anywhere!

Today I will choose to be happy. I will smile at every person I meet. My smile has become my calling card. It is, after all, the most potent weapon I possess. My smile has the strength to forge bonds, break ice, and calm storms. I will use my smile constantly. Because of my smile, the people with whom I come in contact on a daily basis will choose to further my causes and follow my leadership. I will always smile first. That particular display of a good attitude will tell others what I expect in return. My smile is the key to my emotional makeup. A wise man once said, "I do not sing because I am happy; I am happy because I sing!" When I choose to smile, I become the master of my emotions. Discouragement, despair, frustration, and fear will always wither when confronted by my smile. The power of who I am is displayed when I smile.

Today I will choose to be happy. I am the possessor of a grateful spirit. In the past, I have found discouragement in particular situations, until I compared the condition of my life to others less fortunate. Just as a fresh breeze cleans smoke from the air, so does a grateful spirit remove the cloud of despair. It is impossible for the seeds of depression to take root in a thankful heart. My God has bestowed upon me many gifts, and for these I will remember to be grateful. Too many times I have offered up the prayers of a beggar, always asking for more and forgetting my thanks. I do not wish to be seen as a greedy child, unappreciative, and disrespectful. I am grateful for sight and sound and breath. If ever in my life there is a pouring out of blessings beyond that, then I will be grateful for the miracle of abundance.

I will greet each day with laughter. I will smile at every person I meet. I am the possessor of a grateful spirit.

~ Andy Andrews

Decision 6 — The Compassionate Decision

I will greet this day with a forgiving spirit!

For too long, every ounce of forgiveness I owned was locked away, hidden from view, waiting for me to bestow its precious presence upon some worthy person. Alas, I found most people to be singularly un-worthy of my valuable forgiveness and, since they never asked for any, I kept it all for myself. Now, the forgiveness that I hoarded has sprouted inside my heart like a crippled seed yielding bitter fruit.

No more! At this moment, my life has taken on new hope and assurance. Of the entire world's population, I am one of the few posses-sors of the secret to dissipating anger and resentment. I now understand that forgiveness only has value when it is given away. By the simple act of granting forgiveness, I release the demons of the past about which I can do nothing and create in myself a new heart, a new beginning.

I will greet this day with a forgiving spirit. I will forgive even those who do not ask for forgiveness. Many are the times when I have seethed in anger at a word or deed thrown into my life by an unthinking or uncaring person. Valuable hours have been wasted imagining revenge or confrontation. Now I see the truth revealed about this psychological rock inside my shoe. The rage I nurture is often one-sided, for my offender seldom gives thought to his offense!

I will now and forevermore silently offer my forgiveness even to those who do not see that they need it. By the act of forgiving, I am no longer consumed by unproductive thoughts. My bitterness is given up. I am con-tented in my soul and effective again with my fellow man.

I will greet this day with a forgiving spirit. I will forgive those who criticize me unjustly.

Knowing that slavery, in any form, is wrong, I also know that the person who lives a life according to the opinion of others is a slave. I am not a slave. I have chosen my own counsel. I know the difference between right and wrong. I know what is best for the future of my family, and neither misguided opinion nor unjust criticism will alter my course.

Those who are critical of my goals and dreams simply do not understand the higher purpose to which T have been called. Therefore, their scorn does not affect my attitude or action. I forgive their lack of vision and forge ahead. I now know that criticism is part of the price paid for leaping past mediocrity.

I will greet this day with a forgiving spirit. I will forgive myself. For many years, my greatest enemy has been myself. Every mistake, every miscalculation, every stumble I made has been replayed over and over in my mind. Every broken promise, every day wasted, every goal not reached has compounded the disgust I feel for the lack of achievement in my life. My dismay has developed a paralyzing grip. When I disappoint myself, I respond with inaction and become more disappointed.

I realize today that it is impossible to fight an enemy living in my head. By forgiving myself, I erase the doubts, fears, and frustration that have kept my past in the present. From this day forward, my history will cease to control my destiny. I have forgiven myself. My life has just begun.

I will forgive even those who do not ask for forgiveness. I will forgive those who criticize me unjustly. I will forgive myself.

~ Andy Andrews

Decision 7 — The Persistent Decision

I will persist without exception!

Knowing that I have already made changes in my life that will last forever, today I insert the final piece of the puzzle. I possess the greatest power ever bestowed upon mankind, the power of choice. Today, I choose to persist without exception. No longer will I live in a dimension of distraction, my focus blown hither and yon like a leaf on a blustery day. I know the outcome I desire. I hold fast to my dreams. I stay the course. I do not quit.

I will persist without exception. I will continue despite exhaustion. I acknowledge the fact that most people quit when exhaustion sets in. I am not "most people." I am stronger than most people. Average people accept exhaustion as a matter of course. I do not. Average people compare themselves with other people. That is why they are average. I compare myself to my potential. I am not average. I see exhaustion as a precursor to victory.

How long must a child try to walk before he actually does so? Do I not have more strength than a child? More understanding? More desire? How long must I work to succeed before I actually do so? A child would never ask the question, for the answer does not matter. By persisting without exception, my outcome—my success—is assured. I will persist without exception. I focus on results.

To achieve the results I desire, it is not even necessary that I enjoy the process. It is only important that I continue the process with my eyes on the outcome. An athlete does not enjoy the pain of training; an athlete enjoys the results of having trained. A young falcon is pushed from the nest, afraid and tumbling from the cliff. The pain of learning to fly cannot be an enjoyable experience, but the anguish of learning to fly is quickly forgotten as the falcon soars to the heavens.

A sailor who fearfully watches stormy seas lash his vessel will always steer an unproductive course. But a wise and experienced captain keeps his eye firmly fixed upon the lighthouse. He knows that by guiding his ship directly to a specific point, the time spent in discomfort is lessened. And by keeping his eye on the light, there never exists one second of discouragement. My light, my harbor, my future is within sight!

I will persist without exception. I am a person of great faith. In Jeremiah, my Creator declares, "For I know the plans I have for you, plans to prosper you and not to harm you, plans to give you hope and a future." From this day forward, I will claim a faith in the certainty of my future. Too much of my life has been spent doubting my beliefs and believing my doubts. No more! I have faith in my future. I do not look left or right. I look forward. I can only persist.

For me, faith will always be a sounder guide than reason because reason can only go so far—faith has no limits. I will expect miracles in my life because faith produces them every day. I will believe in the future that I do not see. That is faith. And the reward of this faith is to see the future that I believed.

I will continue despite exhaustion. I focus on results. I am a person of great faith.

~ Andy Andrews

Maturity Defined

Maturity is many things. First, it is the ability to base a judgment on the big picture, the long haul.

It means being able to pass up "fun for the minute" and select the course of action that will pay off later. One of the characteristics of infancy is the "I want it now" approach. Grown up people can wait.

Maturity is the ability to stick with a project or a situation until it has been completed. The adult who is constantly changing jobs, changing friends and changing spouses is immature. He cannot stick it out be-cause he has not grown up. Everything seems to turn sour (or uninteresting) after a while.

Maturity is the capacity to face unpleasantness, frustration, discomfort and defeat without complaint or collapse. The mature person knows he can't have everything his own way. Life won't allow it. He is able to defer to circumstances, to other people, and to time.

Maturity is the ability to live up to your responsibilities and keep your word. This means being dependable. Dependability equates with person-al integrity. Do you mean what you say and say what you mean?

The world if filled with people who can't be counted on. They never seem to come through in the crunch. They are the cop-outs who break promises and substitute alibis for performance. Invariably they show up late, or not at all. They are confused and disorganized. Their lives are a chaotic maze of unfinished business.

Maturity is the ability to make a decision and stand by it. Immature people spend most of their time exploring endless possibilities and then they do nothing. Action requires courage. And there can be no maturity without courage.

~ Ann Landers

If

If you can keep your head when all about you
Are losing theirs and blaming it on you;
If you can trust yourself when all men doubt you,
But, make allowance for their doubting too.
If you can wait and not be tired by waiting,
Or being hated, don't give way to hating,
And yet don't look too good, nor talk too wise.

If you can dream, and not make dreams your master,
If you can think, and not make thoughts your air,
If you can meet with triumph and disaster,
And treat those two impostors just the same,
If you can bear to hear the truth you've spoken,
Twisted by knaves to make a trap for fools,
Or watch the things you've given your life to, broken,
And stoop and build 'em up with worn out tools.

If you can make one heap of all your winnings,
And risk it on one turn of "pitch and toss,"
And lose and start again at your beginnings,
And never breathe a word about your loss,
If you can force your heart and nerve and sinew,
To serve your turn long after they are gone,
And hold on when there is nothing in you,
Except the "will" which says to them: "Hold On!"

If you can talk with crowds and keep your virtue,
Or walk with kings, nor lose the common touch,
If neither foes nor loving friends can hurt you,
If all men count with you, but none too much,
If you can fill the unforgiving minute,
With sixty seconds worth of distance run,
Your is the Earth and everything that's in it,
And, which is more; you'll be a Man, my son!

~ Rudyard Kipling

Class

    Class never runs scared. It is sure-footed and confident in the knowledge that you can meet life head on and handle whatever comes along. Jacob's wrestling match with the angel—those with class have wrestled with their own personal angel and it marks them thereafter.
    Class never makes excuses. It takes its lumps and learns from past mistakes. Class is considerate of others. It knows that good manners are

nothing more than a series of good petty sacrifices. Class bespeaks an aristocracy that has nothing to do with ancestors or money. The most affluent blue-blood can be totally without class, while the descendant of a Welsh miner may ooze class from every pore. Class never tries to build itself up by tearing others down.

Class is already up and need not strive to look better by making others worse. Class can walk with kings and keep its virtue and talk with crowds and keep the common touch.

Everyone is comfortable with a person who has class because he is comfortable with himself. If you have class, you don't need much of anything else. If you don't have it, no matter what else you have, it doesn't make much difference.

The Average Man

The world is "NOT" looking for the average man
One content to live off the fat of the land
Who like the tree with the one dead limb
Never uses the full talents God has given him.

The world is "NOT" looking for the average man
Who is willing to quit just because he can
And to be satisfied with being better than some
Not giving a thought about improvement to come.

The world is "NOT" looking for the average man
Who finds it an honor with the mediocre to stand
And finishes the race in the middle of the pack
While the world goes on and never looks back.

The world "IS" looking for the champion man
Who will give his all whenever he can
And no matter what the cost, he will do his best
Never to be content with being like the rest.

The world "IS" looking for the champion man

Who has the toughness of a calloused hand
Who is busy at work to improve his skill
That he might escape being "run of the mill."

The world "IS" looking for the champion man
Who won't say "I can't," but will say "I can"
Who finishes the race in front of the pack
So intent in his effort he never looks back.

So to you who are preparing for your life's work
Who never intend your job to shirk
Remember, the champion man could be you
But only your best will ever do.

Every human being, for vitality, maturity, growth and fulfillment needs a constant risk, constant stress in order to reach his fulfillment as a creature. When you play it safe, as so many people try to do—get a job and bury themselves in the soft amorphous womb of industry or some giant corporation—quite often you lose the qualities that make a human being great or successful. You tend to relax, you tend to stop growing.

To comprehend a man's life, it is necessary to know what he does but also what he purposely leaves undone. There is a limit to the amount of work that can be gotten out of a human body or a human brain; and he is a wise man who wastes no energy on pursuits for which he is not fitted. And he is still wiser, who, among the things he can do well, resolutely follows his best.

❖

Worldly Success

Natural talent, intelligence, a wonderful education—none of these guarantee success. Something else is needed; the sensitivity to understand what other people want and the willingness to give it to them. Worldly success depends on pleasing others. No one is going to win fame, recognition, or advancement just because he or she thinks it is deserved. Someone else has to think so too.

~ John Luther

We Learn and Retain:

10% of what we hear
15% of what we see
20% of what we both see and hear
40% of what we discuss with others
80% of what we experience directly or practice
90% of what we attempt to teach others

Life is the "Now"

We can only accomplish one thing at a time. If we are truly convinced of this reality, we'll relax and concentrate with full awareness and responsiveness. After a while, the enjoyment of the present moment will become a habit. So forget the failure of yesterday and the anxiety of tomorrow. Life is the now. Live intensely.

And venture into each day.

We must STOP – LOOK – LISTEN. Be alert! What's happening to me right now? Am I feeling the total experience of this moment?

To amass great ideas and have healthy emotions is a far more enriching experience than amassing money.

Someone once said, "Money is like manure—when it is in a pile it stinks, but when it is spread around it helps life grow." Life is more than a savings account to be fought over after our death.

Now is the time to cash our money out into experiences. We cannot afford to bankrupt our mind and emotions.

How to Improve Without Any Physical Effort

Answer: Concentration
Concentration is defined by 4 words.
The first two are "LOOK" and "SEE"
LOOK
Everyone looks!
SEE
Very few people see! For example: seeing the open person on both sides of the court; seeing the open player in transition; seeing when a teammate needs help on defense, etc. The list is endless. Improving our ability to see will make us a better team.
The second two are "HEAR" and "LISTEN"
HEAR
Everyone hears!
LISTEN
Few people listen! What is being said? What are we being told? What is being said to a teammate? What is expected of me in my role(s) on the team? By improving your listening ability, you will become a better player.
Concentration leads to anticipation, which leads to recognition, which leads to reaction, which leads to execution!

Common Ignorance

I saw some men in my hometown. I saw them knocking a building down with a heave and a ho and a mighty yell. They swung a beam and the side wall fell, and I said to the boss, "Are these men skilled—the type you would hire if you wanted to build?" He laughed and said, "Why, no, indeed, common ignorance is all I need. For with ignorance I can tear down in a day or two what it took a skilled builder a lifetime to do." And I thought to myself as I walked away, which of the roles am I going to play?

~ Lou Holtz

The Indispensable Man

Sometime when you're feeling important
Sometime when your ego's in bloom
Sometime when you take it for granted
You're the best qualified in the room.

Sometime when you feel that you're going
Would leave an unfilled hole
Just follow this simple instruction
And see how it humbles your soul.

Take a bucket and fill it with water
Put your hand in it up to the wrist,
Pull it out, and the hole that's remaining
Is the measure of how you'll be missed.

You may splash all you please when you enter
You can stir up the water galore
But, stop and you'll find in a minute
That it looks quite the same as before.

The moral in this quaint example
Is to do just the best that you can
Be proud of yourself, but remember,
There is no indispensable man!

No One is Perfect

Johnny had been bad and was sent to his room. After a while he emerged and informed his mother that he had thought it over and said a prayer.

"Fine," said the pleased mother. "If you ask God to make you good,

He will help you."

"Oh, I didn't ask him to help me be good," replied Johnny. "I asked him to help you put up with me."

Boys will be boys, as the old saying goes, and it's a wise mother who accepts this fact.

The same acceptance is the better part of wisdom for supervisors and managers too. Few employees are ideal; no more than managers are. And the sooner you accept this fact, the sooner you can get on with the business at hand.

No athletic coach ever coached the perfect team. The challenge is to do the best possible with the material available. The real test of any leader, coach or company president are the results achieved with the personnel available—not what might have been accomplished if all the people were stars.

Excellence is the development of personal potential—not conquest over others.

We are not equal in talent, potential, opportunity, or health, or simple good luck. So we strive for relative excellence by setting realistic goals.

The goal is the most important element of excellence as Seneca so wisely reflected: "When a person does not know what harbor he is making for—no wind is the right wind."

Only two people with the power of reconciliation can venture safety into the experience of mutual, maximum love. When we love others, we put into their hands the power of hurting us. It is human to hurt, and realistic people are prepared for the friction of interaction. The risk of love is in the power of forgiveness and reconciliation.

Love is "not having to say you're sorry." Intimacy will always have its disagreements, but do we have the capacity to be the first to seek out and heal hurt feelings?

This is the true test of reconciliation—to begin again when there appears to be an ending.

We are friends, acquaintances, or strangers who are involved in many lives in a cursory manner. If we are truly glad that others are alive and happy, then we'll convey this joy in the intensity of a few passing moments.

We cannot give the intensity of our love to everyone, but we can give the intensity of the present moment. When we are talking to someone, we should act as though this individual is the only person in the world: anything less than our total awareness and sensitivity will be an injustice to his presence.

Most of our ideas are usually about experiences--what has happened to us or what has happened to others. Our ideas broaden our vision, but only experiences expand our ideas.

Life is never a waste of time if we are experiencing new, healthy ideas of ourselves. Many times these experiences are gained only in disappointment. We might go to bed one evening with the feeling of accomplishing very little. If we take the time to reflect, however, we'll learn something new from every experience that has happened to us.

Sayings

Life is like a ten-speed bike. Most of us have gears we never use.

Those who use time wisely focus on results and not on tasks or activities. They learn to structure their environment so it is conducive to concentration. They learn to distinguish between all the pressing demands on their time and those things that actually require attention. Time is a valuable resource. Unless it is managed well, nothing else can be. And although learning to use time effectively is not an easy task, it is well worth the effort.

❖

It is not enough merely to exist. It is not enough to say, "I am earning enough to live and to support my family. I do my work well. I'm a good father. I'm a good husband. I'm a good churchgoer." That's all very well. But you must do something more. Seek always to do some good, somewhere. Every man has to seek in his own self to be nobler and to realize his own true worth. You must give some time to your fellowman.

~ Albert Schweitzer

❖

Alvin Toffler in *Future Shock* describes the dizzy disorientation that arises from the superimposing of a new culture on an old one. Ideas should grow gradually. If we stop thinking, change will be a shattering experience.

Crisis and confrontation would be useless words if we only called upon continuity. Marriage problems, the generation gap, and the identity crisis would not be a revolution if we continued to evolve and refresh our thinking.

Usually confused action is born from confused ideas. Without adequate thought and preparation, unharnessed activity accomplishes very little.

Our activity then should be guided from a center of reflection deep in the silence of our mind.

❖

When we pause and enjoy silence, we discover answers and clarifications that activity does not have time to reveal. We put ourselves together again.

Take three-minute vacations. To vacate means to empty out. Get rid of your anxieties and tensions. Relax and reenergize. Take time out to stretch; it does wonders for the nervous system.

Once we make the initial decision to deepen our involvement, however, we cannot be afraid to give of ourselves. We truly experience our vitality, our aliveness, our power when we give. Our good intentions cannot remain in the deep recesses of our mind. Along with desire and a sense of risk, participation is the best way to give and get out of ourselves to enjoy life.

"Now" is the time to go out of our way for those who need us. "Yes" is the only protection we have from indifference. Apathy can always find an excuse. It always has a plan to evade involvement. It is false to assume that we'll be happy if we only mind our own business.

Existentialism forms a consciousness that we create ourselves. Unfortunately, it isolates us within our skin. We become preoccupied with our own growth. We pursue our freedom and our authenticity. We are invited to "do our own thing," "do what comes naturally," and "do what we feel is best for ourselves."

Yet, there are times when a healthy relationship does not permit us "to do our own thing." It is absolutely impossible to live in constant harmony with others if we do not think of the common good and adjust our personal feelings accordingly.

Involvement cannot survive without compromise. Adjustment, in the form of compromise—especially when it is sacrificial—is not a sign of weakness. What might be good for me might be harmful to someone else. We cannot talk about our rights if justice is being deprived. We cannot talk about our personal freedom and fulfillment if our quest is only a conquest and our aim is the destruction of another's rights.

If we desire to be happy and at peace today, then we should not turn over the power of manipulation to anyone. Misery enjoys company, and every miserable, bitter, and sarcastic person we meet can manipulate our peaceful life style if we are not careful.

Our best reaction is to remain happy so that they feel uncomfortable being miserable. We will not always find ourselves in a totally comfortable relationship, but the mature person manages to work things out without losing his cool.

No one can satisfy everyone all the time and we'll wear ourselves down with nervous tension if we try. We should build on the premise that everyone is different and thus develop a realistic expectation of how people will react. We cannot expect to live by our convictions and fully satisfy everyone.

❖

Many business people seem to believe that the longer they delay making decisions the more mistakes they will avoid.

"See me later," "I'll think about it," "take it up with me in the fall," "I'm busy now," "wait until times are better," "I'll study it at my leisure." Such are the standard methods by which brain-pain is avoided.

The postponement of matters that should be decided cannot be defended at all. "No," may be the right answer to most propositions that are presented to an executive. The main thing is to decide, to clear the desk, to keep the traffic moving.

❖

No society of nations, no people within a nation, no family can benefit through mutual aid unless good will exceeds ill will; unless the spirit of cooperation surpasses antagonism; unless we all see and act as though the other man's welfare determines our own welfare.

~ Henry Ford II

Kindness may be described in many ways. It is the poetry of the heart, the music of the world. It is a golden chain that binds society together. It is a fountain of gladness. Kind hearts are more than coronets. Kind words produce their own beautiful image in man's soul. Everyone knows the pleasure of receiving a kind look, a warm greeting, and a hand held out in time of need. Such gestures can be made at so little expense, yet they bring such dividends to the investor.

First things must come first. This is the law of priorities, which is necessary for a healthy involvement. With only so much time and energy, we must make a decision of what is most important in our life and concentrate on our choice. With a little humility, we can make realistic expectations and not lose perspective.

Our life has many modes. We cannot live them all because we do not have time. So we make a choice—a particular vocation, wife, friend and hobbies—of available modes. As we emphasize one mode of living, others will fade out and become less important.

"I feel; therefore, I am." A feeling person allows life to penetrate deep into his personality. Reality percolates through every fiber and muscle he experiences.

He savors reality and fully digests real life.

Feeling real life consequently makes us real. We take off the masks and respond with tears, tenderness, touch, or any other emotion that the experience calls forth. Our strength is in our realness.

The secret of becoming a great person is as easy as desiring it; for "desire" means "to wish earnestly, to crave, to yearn, to long for."

There is the story told of a master and his student who was studying a great truth, the student just could not comprehend. In desperation the master grabbed the student and put his head under water. At the very last second the master pulled him from death. He asked the student what he was thinking when he was under water. "I desired air," he answered. The master responded, "So then you must desire truth and you will receive it."

We too must desire to become better than we are, then we will be able to develop our potential.

If we feel worn out and tired, we are probable wasting our energy. There are three major dissipations: association with negative people, thinking negative thoughts, and engaging in negative conversation.

The negative dissipates our vitality and leaves us bored and angry. Jonathan Livingston Seagull discovered that it was specifically these two traits that shortened a gull's life. It will shorten our life too.

❖

The pursuit of "more and multiple" drives us into a dizzy dis-orientation that cries for cop-outs and escapes.

We clutch to ourselves the burden of our many possessions and sink into murky waters of emptiness.

As we suffocate the simple beauty of living, we learn too late that happiness is knowing how to be detached and conserve energy.

❖

If we are dissatisfied with our identity, then we must reevaluate our ideas. We are what we think. Many people will never be at peace because they have not rearranged and simplified their ideas. They take tranquilizers instead of changing their mentality.

❖

Use these eight phrases generously and the experience of love will be magnificent:

I love you
I am sorry
I miss you
I am wrong
Together
We forget
Thank You
I forgive

Our past mistakes and future apprehensions are not considerate of our digestion or sleep--both of which we need to conserve our energy.

Worry dissipates our strength and inhibits the enjoyment and intensity of the present moment.

So break the worry habit; take the risk of being a free person and let God do the worrying. Remember He created you, so rely on His goodness.

❖

When an electric circuit is overloaded, it blows a fuse and leaves the whole house in darkness. We have drained the energy.

Our desires increase more rapidly than our power to produce, and we can easily burn ourselves out with overload. We drain our energy.

We have only so much energy; don't lose it all by overload.

❖

In November of 1970, the police found a young girl who had lived in virtual isolation for 13 years. Still clad in diapers, she had the mind of an infant and could not talk. She had been deprived of receiving ideas which would have set off the dynamic evolution of human personality.

We are all born with the raw material of existence. Human contact and an evolution of ideas gradually nurture human life. Our life then expands as our ideas expand.

Erik Erikson has said, "We cannot have an identity without an ideology." The confusion of who we are—our identity—often keeps us ill-at-ease. We search for the meaning and clarification of the "I" in our life. We ask the questions: What values am I seeking? What really counts for me? How am I coming across to other people?

Our philosophy of life sets the tone for our values and goals. Our life then unifies around this fundamental choice with a consistency that keeps order and meaning in our life. Otherwise, we will become con-fused with thousands of unrelated ideas.

❖

Jim Burtchnell has written that schism is a breakdown in patience before it is a conflict in creed.

Everyone is in a hurry to make conclusions. If we could only slow down and be patient enough to listen, there could be great possibilities for a unity in diversity.

Usually, impatience feeds imprudence, and there is an exchange of distasteful remarks and curt replies. Then the gap becomes larger, and there is little desire to bridge it.

Ideas should be tempered with prudence. A prudent person is quick to think, quick to listen, but slow to speak. He realizes that hasty, rash judgments made by an uninformed mind will only strain emotions and hurt good people. Ideas are too powerful to be rashly spoken.

❖

An electric wire is a very quiet and unassuming dynamism. Touch it and its electrifying current fills our body. An idea has that same power.

Electricity brings us warmth, refreshment, and life, but it can also kill. An idea likewise can destroy us. It did Hitler and Charles Manson. Yet, it is also the source of a fruitful and exciting life.

An ideology is powerful, so we must temper it with the Christian message of love. We should ask the question: are our ideas creating or destroying?

❖

The Book of Proverbs stirs our conscience when it says:

Do not refuse a kindness to anyone who asks it if it is in your power to perform it. Do not say, "Go away, come another time! I will give it to you tomorrow" if you can do it now.

We cannot afford to become an "if only" person constantly promising "if only the conditions were right." If we can say, "yes," then say it "now" and get involved.

❖

To be with "it" and "right on" are contemporary idioms associated with involvement. They are real words that speak action. They give the feeling that we are in the middle of something important.

Yet involvement must be tempered with solitude if we are to succeed. Adrian van Kaam warns us:

No involvement is possible without detachment, and no detachment is meaningful without a deepening of involvement.

We must occasionally leave the world of involvement to reevaluate the reasons for being involved. Detachment purifies our motives and refreshes our integrity.

When our ideology becomes a selfish pursuit of "pennies, power and prestige," then it will ultimately destroy us. Detachment is the only guardian of our sanity. It keeps our ideas in proper perspective and keeps us "right on."

Pettiness endangers potential because it causes boredom. It drains our life of wonderment, enthusiasm, risk and expansion. When we expand and broaden our personality, we allow a whole new experience of adventure to come pouring in.

Many people are ill content because they are just not excited about anything. They have stopped learning. They have a paucity of ideas and interests, and therefore they have little motivation. They live their day with petty conversation and superficial activity.

One cure for boredom is a constant pursuit of learning. Knowledge refreshes the mind, recreates the spirit and motivates the body. It creates the enthusiasm and desire to live an exciting and full day in spite of routine.

Life is not dull. We make it dull by limiting our potential and stifling our interests with pettiness.

Being criticized is not a problem if you develop a positive way of dealing with it. Winston Churchill had the following words of Abe Lincoln framed on the wall of his office: "I do the very best I can. I mean to keep going. If the end brings me out all right, then what is said against me won't matter. If I am wrong, ten angels swearing I was right won't make a difference."

One is happy as a result of one's own efforts once one knows the necessary ingredients of happiness: simple tastes, a certain degree of courage, self-denial to a point, love of work, and above all, a clear conscience.

~ Mary Ann Evans

Every idea is a cause that has an effect. What we think usually makes us what we are. If we are ashamed of what we are becoming, then we should evaluate our ideas.

We cannot determine our destiny, but we do have a choice of an ideology that will influence the direction of our life. We need not be a prisoner of hopeless boredom. The key to freedom and growth is an idea.

"Agere sequitur esse" is a Latin phrase which is translated to mean: "How you act follows what you are."

If we are ashamed of our actions, then we should reevaluate our ideas and probe our feelings. Our identity is a natural product of our ideology. We are our ideas so we should be comfortable with them.

Who, then, is the loneliest one? It is the person who is not at home with his own thoughts, the one who is alien to his own feelings, the one who is a stranger to himself—he is the loneliest person of all.

~ Arthur Jersild

No one will ever get out of this world alive. Resolve therefore to maintain a reasonable sense of values.

Take care of yourself. Good health is everyone's major source of wealth. Without it, happiness is almost impossible.

❖

Resolve to be cheerful and helpful. People will repay you in kind.

❖

Avoid angry, abrasive persons. They are generally vengeful.

❖

Avoid zealots. They are generally humorless.

❖

Resolve to listen more and to talk less. No one ever learns anything by talking.

❖

Be wary of giving advice. Wise men don't need it and fools won't heed it.

❖

Resolve to be tender with the young, compassionate with the aged, sympathetic with the striving and tolerant of the weak and the wrong. Sometime in life you will have been all of these.

❖

Do not equate money with success. There are many successful mon-eymakers who are miserable failures as human beings. What counts most about success is how a person achieves it.

IX

TWENTY SECOND SERMONS

People fall into two categories —
pretenders or contenders.
Who are you?

20 Second Sermons

The future is purchased by the present!

❖

If you don't care where you are going, any road will get you there!

❖

You can't direct the wind, but you can adjust your sails!

❖

No one knows less than the one who knows it all!

❖

Imagination is more important than knowledge!
~ Albert Einstein

❖

The important thing is not to stop questioning!
~ Albert Einstein

❖

Chance favors the prepared mind!
~ Louis Pasteur

❖

Success is more attitude than aptitude!

❖

The desire to succeed means nothing without the will to prepare!

❖

Failure is the path of least persistence!

❖

Great minds have purposes; little minds have wishes.
Little minds are subdued by misfortunes; great minds rise above them.

~ Washington Irving

❖

When you are making a success of something, it's not work, it's a way of life. You enjoy yourself because you are making your contribution to the world.

~ Andy Granatelli

❖

All the great things are simple, and many can be expressed in a single word:
Freedom, Justice, Honor, Duty, Mercy, Hope

~ Winston Churchill

❖

Self-centered people are the ones who spend so much time talking about themselves that we never get a chance to talk about ourselves.

❖

Respect cannot be learned, purchased, or acquired—
it can only be earned.

❖

A professor who had been teaching for years was counseling a newcomer to the profession.

"You'll notice," she said, "that in every class you teach there will be at least one student who wants to argue with everything you say. Your reaction will probably be to silence him immediately. But think twice about doing that, he may be the only one who is listening to you!"

❖

We often act as though comfort and luxury were the chief requirements of life, when what we really need to make us happy is something to be enthusiastic about.

❖

The greatest of all faults is to be conscious of none.
~ Caryle

❖

The difference between a successful career and a mediocre one sometimes consists of leaving about four or five things a day unsaid.

❖

Nothing is interesting if you're not interested.

❖

If you're feeling low, don't despair. The sun has a sinking spell every night, but it comes back up every morning.

❖

If you want a place in the sun, you have to put up with a few blisters.
~ Abigail Van Buren

The way I see it, if you want the rainbow, you gotta put up with the rain.
                                                                    ~ Dolly Parton

❖

Bad weather always looks worse through a window.

❖

The best preparation for tomorrow is to do today's work superbly well.
                                                                    ~ Sir William Osler

❖

It's tough to climb the ladder of success, especially if you're trying to keep your nose to the grindstone, your shoulder to the wheel, your eye on the ball, and your ear to the ground.

❖

The Lord gave us two ends--one to sit on and the other to think with. Success depends on which one we use the most.
                                                                    ~ Ann Landers

❖

The one thing that most of us do better than anyone else is read our own writing.

❖

Opportunities multiply as they are seized; die when neglected.

❖

The trouble with advice is that you seldom know whether it is good or bad until you no longer need it.

❖

Tact is the ability to raise your eyebrows instead of the roof.

❖

If you have your sight, you are blessed,
If you have insight, you are a thousand times blessed.

❖

The trouble with self-made men is that they worship their creator.

❖

The trouble with this world is that too many people go through life with a catcher's mitt on both hands.

❖

Most of us will never do great things,
but we can do small things in a great way.

❖

Thinking is the hardest work there is;
probably the reason why so few engage in it.

~ Henry Ford

❖

The toughest test of self-control is to listen to someone describing the same ailment you have and not mention it.

❖

Experience is what you get when you were expecting something else.

❖

Life is like riding a bicycle. You don't fall off unless you stop peddling.
~ Claude Pepper

❖

A man is never astonished that he doesn't know what another does, but he is surprised at the gross ignorance of the other in not knowing what he does.
~ Haliburton

❖

Find something you love to do and you'll never work a day in your life.
~ Harvey Mackay

❖

There is nothing wrong with having nothing to say, unless you insist on saying it.

❖

What people don't say is often as important as what they do. When people don't talk to you, they're trying to tell you something.

❖

When a person lowers his voice, he wants something; when he raises it, it's a sign he didn't get it.

❖

The real fault is to have faults and not try to mend them.
~ Confucius

There is a chord in every heart that has a sigh in it if you use the right touch.

❖

Peace is not made at the council table or by treaties, but in the hearts of men.

~ Herbert Hoover

❖

Peace comes not from the absence of conflict in life but from the ability to cope with it.

❖

Make each day useful and cheerful and prove that you know the worth of time by employing it well. Then youth will be happy, elders will be without regret, and life will be a beautiful success.

~ Louisa May Alcott

❖

You can give without loving, but you can't love without giving.

❖

I have a very strong feeling that the opposite of love is not hate. It's apathy. It is not giving a damn.

~ Dr. Leo Buscaglia

❖

The psychic task that a person can and must set for himself is not to feel secure but to be able to tolerate insecurity.

~ Erich Fromm

We must view young people not as empty bottles to be filled, but as candles to be lit.

~ Robert H. Shaffer

❖

You would never envy if you would but realize the accumulated power that comes by profiting from the success of other people. Be glad of the big luck of somebody else. Be wise enough to let its inspiration lift you up. Individual success is not stationary. It has no limitations. Congratulate your friend today and he or she may be put in the position to congratulate you tomorrow and be happy for the chance.

~ George Matthew Adams

❖

Friendship should not be thought of as something we get;
It is something we give.

❖

You are not really successful until someone claims he sat beside you in school.

❖

A high school teacher displayed the following
Notice on her bulletin board:
"Free—every Monday through Friday—knowledge.
Bring your own containers."

❖

The more push you have the less pull you need.
Every person who has been successful has been a self-starter.

❖

Enthusiasm makes ordinary people extraordinary.

❖

Fame and fortune ought to add up to something more than fame and fortune.
~ Robert Fulgham

❖

Happiness is more often remembered than experienced.

❖

Be thankful for problems. If they were less difficult, someone with less ability might have your job.

❖

Beware of half-truths. You many have gotten the wrong half.

❖

Four Little Words that aren't heard often enough--
You may be right!

❖

If I had to say in one word what makes a good manager, I'd say decisiveness. You can use the fanciest computers to gather the numbers, but in the end you have to set a timetable and act.
~ Lee Iacocca

❖

My grandfather once told me that there are two kinds of people: those who do the work and those who take the credit. He told me to try to be in the first group; there was less competition there.
~ Indira Gandhi

❖

Small deeds done are better than great deeds planned.
--Peter Marshall

❖

Friendship is like a bank account, you can't continue to draw on it without making a deposit.

❖

If you can't get people to listen any other way, tell them it's confidential. And if you've ever been frustrated or insulted when some-body wouldn't listen to you, then you know how important it is to be a good listener.

❖

Any faucet can turn the water on, but after a few years only a good faucet will turn it off. The same thing applies to human tongues.

❖

A road map will tell us everything we want to know except how to fold it up again.

❖

If you plant a tree, don't keep pulling it up by the roots to see how it's growing.

❖

Temper is what gets most of us into trouble. Pride is what keeps us there.

❖

It is a universal law. The other line moves faster.

❖

Rodney Dangerfield continued to be a loser. When he went to the beach one summer, he said, "I put a seashell to my ear and got a busy signal."

❖

He who loses his head is usually the last one to miss it.

❖

A person wrapped up in himself makes a very small package.

❖

Be bold in what you stand for and careful what you fall for.

❖

If you think education is expensive, try ignorance.

❖

It's what we do, not what we say we believe, that shows what we really think.

❖

Any man can be a father, but it takes a special man to be a dad.

❖

Shine like a glowworm if you can't be a star.

❖

What your eyes don't see, your heart doesn't grieve over.

❖

Shadows fall behind when we walk toward the light.

❖

Any man convinced against his will is of the same opinion still.

❖

A mule dressed in a tuxedo is still a mule.

❖

A penny for your thoughts is now a quarter.

❖

Too many people buy things on the "lay-awake" plan.

❖

More people get run down by gossip than by cars.

❖

Those who aim at nothing always hit it.

❖

Love reduces friction to a fraction.

❖

Praise is a debt we owe to the virtues of others.

❖

A thing worth doing is worth starting.

❖

Money will buy a good dog, but only kindness will make its tail wag.

❖

He who sows thorns should never go barefoot.

❖

Real love stories never have endings.

❖

A friend is a present you give yourself.

❖

It's the traveling bee that gets the honey.

❖

Macho does not prove mucho.

❖

Take sour grapes with a grain of salt.

❖

Faults are thick where love is thin.

❖

Keep your temper, nobody wants it.

❖

No one becomes dizzy from doing good turns.

❖

Always proofread your work to see that you didn't leave any words out.

❖

If it's going to be, it's up to me.

❖

Nothing great was ever accomplished without enthusiasm.

❖

Confidence is what happens when you've done the hard work that entitles you to succeed.

❖

You can't always be the most talented person in the room;
but you can be the most competitive.

❖

You can't always control what happens;
but you can control how you handle it.

❖

The future belongs to those who believe in the beauty of their dreams.

❖

The whole world won't recognize your ability until you demonstrate it.

❖

To accomplish great things we must not only act, but also dream; not only plan, but also believe.

❖

The world is full of willing people, some willing to work, and others willing to let them.

❖

The only place where success comes before work is in the dictionary.

❖

The will to win is important, but the will to prepare is vital.

❖

Adversity causes some people to break, others to break records.

❖

If you can dream it, you can do it.

❖

The greatest thrill in life comes when you accomplish something others never thought possible.

❖

In order to win or succeed, you must always take the chance of losing.

❖

Sometimes, the best thing to get off your chest is your chin.

❖

Lord, grant me that I may always desire more than I can accomplish.

❖

Although where you come from is not nearly as important as where you are going, he is a wise man who never forgets.

❖

There's no use itching for something unless you're willing to scratch for it.

❖

Obstacles are what you see when you take your eyes of the goal.

❖

When you're in any contest, regardless of the score, you should work to the very last minute as if there were a chance to lose.

❖

It's easier to do the job right rather than explain why you didn't do it all.

❖

The manly man is the one who always finds excuses for others but never for himself.

❖

The noble secret of laughing at oneself is the greatest humor of all.

❖

Average is just as close to the bottom as it is to the top.

❖

Shoot for the moon; if you miss, you will land among the stars.

❖

Food for Thought:
Three essential ingredients in the recipe for a happier family life are
Prayer – Patience - Understanding

❖

Home is where you don't have to make reservations in advance.

❖

When life throws you a curve, it's to teach you how to bend.

❖

God without man is still GOD. Man without God is nothing.

❖

Don't use a gallon of words to express a spoonful of thought.

❖

You can't get much done by starting tomorrow.

❖

Our greatest fault is being conscious of others' faults.

❖

That's the problem with a garden—the fruits of your labor are vegetables.

❖

When friends meet, hearts warm.

❖

If it is so beautifully arranged on the plate, you know someone's fingers have been all over it.

❖

The only commodity that doesn't deteriorate with use is knowledge.

❖

Among the fastest things in the world is the tape coming out of a supermarket cash register.

❖

What a piece of bread looks like depends on whether you are hungry or not.

❖

It is not the food in your life that counts; it's the life in your food.

❖

Never put a question mark where God puts a period.

❖

Hospitality—the virtue which induces us to feed and lodge certain people who are not in need of food and lodging.

❖

When it comes to decorating, Mother Nature has the greatest taste.

❖

Stress is like an ice cream cone, you have to learn to lick it.

❖

The secret to enjoying life is to be thankful for what each day brings.

❖

If you have given up trying to open something, tell a 4-year old not to touch it.

❖

The key to everything is patience; you get the chicken by hatching the egg, not by smashing it.

❖

Attitudes are contagious, make yours worth catching.

❖

No person is lonely while eating spaghetti; it requires much attention.

❖

People may fail many times, but they become failures only when they begin to blame others.

❖

If yesterday's deeds look big, you haven't done much today.

❖

Nothing improves one's prayer life faster than big trouble.

❖

If you must cry over spilled milk, condense it.

❖

Opportunist – someone who, finding himself in hot water, decides to take a bath.

❖

Happiness is like jam--you can't spread even a little without getting some on yourself.

❖

Starting from scratch isn't as bad as starting without it.

❖

A sense of humor is like a needle and thread—it will patch up many things.

❖

Often we look so long at the closed door that we do not see the one which has been opened for us.

❖

Watch your pennies, the government will take care of your dollars.

❖

The most comfortable sleeping position is the one you find after turning off the alarm.

❖

Tact is the ability to raise your eyebrows instead of the roof.

❖

A house is a home when it provides food and warmth for the soul as well as the body.

❖

Hope and pray for a stronger back—not lighter burdens.

❖

Do the dreaded job first so you'll have all day to look forward to.

❖

I

If you are going to be blue, be bright blue.

❖

Giving does not drain our resources, but provides a space for us to refill.

❖

Hospitality means treat your company like family and your family like company.

❖

The secret of contentment is knowing how to enjoy what you have.

❖

Variety may be the spice of life, but monotony buys the groceries.

❖

A new broom sweeps clean but the old one knows the corners.

❖

Any trouble too small to take to God is too small to worry about.

❖

Life is like a buffet line—there aren't any waiters, so you have to help yourself.

❖

A wishbone isn't the substitute for a backbone.

❖

If you tickle the earth with a hoe, she laughs at you with a harvest.

❖

What is learned with pleasure is never forgotten.

❖

You can always make an easy task more difficult by doing it with reluctance.

❖

A rose smells better than cabbage but it will not make a better soup.

❖

Through all the changing scenes of life, in trouble and in joy, The praises of my God shall still my heart and tongue.

❖

It is neither wealth nor splendor, but tranquility and occupation that gives you happiness.

❖

Yesterday's the past – tomorrow the future – but today is a gift; which is why it is called the "present".

❖

Snap judgments have a way of becoming unfastened.

❖

What counts are not the things you do at Christmas time, but the Christmas things you do all the time.

❖

You can disagree without being disagreeable.

❖

Success is getting what you want; happiness is wanting what you get.

You don't have to stamp out someone else's light to make yours shine brighter.

❖

There is no right way to do a wrong thing.

❖

When there is nothing left but God, we find that God is enough.

❖

Let disappointment become your strength instead of your downfall.

❖

Use the past as a springboard instead of a hammock.

❖

Anger can speed up your mouth as much as it slows down your brain.

❖

People don't plan to fail; they fail to plan.

❖

A success that tastes sour instead of sweet probably is more of a failure.

❖

Some people are so busy preparing for a rainy day that they miss the sunshine.

❖

Treat your mind as respectfully as your body; if you fill it with garbage it doesn't work as well as it should.

❖

Health is the thing that makes you feel that now is the best time of the year.

❖

Know yourself and your neighbor will not mistake you.

❖

Volunteering to help others makes your problems seem smaller.

❖

If I cannot do great things, I can do small things in a great way.

❖

The best thing you can give your children is time.

❖

Instead of counting the days, make the days count.

❖

We are all dispensable.

❖

People can be categorized three ways:

Those who make things happen
Those who watch things happen

Those who wonder what happened.
Where do you fit in?

❖

Self-discipline is as important as a good attitude in reaching a goal.

❖

The Olympics show us that people still exist who can discipline themselves, and have a commitment to excellence.

❖

A team is only as strong as its weakest link.

❖

Be organized! Use a time management schedule, have a wristwatch and do what you are supposed to do and be where you are supposed to be.

❖

Be part of the solution, not part of the problem.

❖

The word "fair" is always used by players and parents as a quality they want most in a coach, yet sometimes it is the quality they, themselves, least possess.

❖

Be responsible! Be on time! Keep your word!

❖

Happiness is what you make it.

❖

Despite all of the advice from your parents, coaches and teachers— you are on your own when it comes to the choices you make. Can you be trusted?

❖

The top three universal questions and answers are: Can I trust you? (Do what is right.) Are you committed to excellence? (Be the best you can be.) Are you sincere? (Treat others as you want to be treated.)

❖

Nothing will work unless you do.
~ John Wooden

❖

Generally speaking, individual performances don't win basketball games.
~ John Wooden

❖

The harder you prepare, the luckier you get.
~ Michael Jordan

❖

It's a battle of wills, not a battle of skills.
~ Isiah Thomas

❖

Four corners of success—commitment, effort, motivation, discipline

~ Don King

❖

Play the game, the officials will referee.
~ Don King

❖

When you make a mistake, there are only three things you should ever do about it: Admit it – Learn from it – Don't repeat it.
~ Paul "Bear" Bryant

❖

To improve the team, improve yourself.
~ Rick Synold

❖

"Well done is better than well said.
~ Benjamin Franklin

❖

People, like nails, lose the effectiveness when they lose direction and begin to bend.
~ Walter Savage Landor

❖

Passivity invites mediocrity, while aggressiveness makes its own breaks.
~ George Raveling

❖

Successful players/teams are willing to do the little things that the underachieving players/teams don't.

~ Dan Lier

❖

Failures are expected by losers, ignored by winners.
~ John Gibbs

❖

Hard work will not guarantee you anything, but without it you don't stand a chance.
~ Pat Riley

❖

How do you respond to the challenge in the second half will determine what you become after the game, whether you are a winner or a loser.
~ Lou Holtz

❖

I don't look for excuses when we lose, and I don't buy excuses when we win.
--Dave Cowens

❖

I'm a great believer in luck, and I find the harder I work, the more I have of it.
~ Thomas Jefferson

❖

It's not up to anyone else to make me give my best.
~ Hakeem Olajuwon

❖

Nothing in the world can take the place of persistence. Talent will not.

Nothing is more common than unsuccessful men with talent.

❖

Don't wait for your ship to come in. . . swim out to it.

❖

Do not count the days, make the days count.

❖

Winners are never surprised to win; losers are never surprised to lose. A winner listens; a loser just waits until it's their turn to talk.

❖

Cooperation – a word consisting of eleven letters that can be spelled with two: W-E.

❖

When a winner makes a mistake, they say, "I was wrong." When a loser makes a mistake, they say, "It wasn't my fault."

❖

The ability to beat the odds lies within all of us.

❖

Success will come to those who wait, as long as they work while they wait.

❖

Morale is the first step toward a successful season.

❖

Every sacrifice you make builds character. People with average skills often obtain greatness because they are willing to pay a price for it.

❖

You might not have more talent than your opponent, but you can beat them if you out work them.

❖

Championship teams are made when each player is committed to his teammates' success.

❖

You will only succumb to stress if you are ill prepared.

❖

Will you be the hunter or the hunted?

❖

Momentum is nothing more than a state of mind. . . again an attitude.

❖

Your attitude has the power to change your life. Lincoln, Jordan, Armstrong, Edison – 5,000 failures before success.

❖

Everyday ordinary people do extraordinary things—Today is your day.

The best part of getting knocked down is getting back up.

❖

Do not be afraid of failure – there is no such thing.

❖

Do not let what you don't have keep you from using what you do have.

❖

You will win the minute you get rid of excuses as to why you can't win and stop wallowing is self-pity!

❖

Made in the USA
Middletown, DE
14 August 2015